EVALUATION:

RELATING TRAINING TO
BUSINESS PERFORMANCE

EVALUATION:

RELATING TRAINING TO BUSINESS PERFORMANCE

Terence Jackson

KOGAN
PAGE

First published in Great Britain in 1989 by Kogan Page Ltd,
120 Pentonville Road, London N1 9JN

Printed and bound in Great Britain by
Richard Clay Ltd, The Chaucer Press, Bungay, Suffolk

British Library Cataloguing in Publication Data

Jackson, Terence
    Evaluation.
    1. Personnel. Training. Effectiveness. Assessment
    I. Title
    658.3'12404

ISBN 1-85091-753-1

Contents

Preface

At the time of writing, training and development is fashionable. Companies and public sector organizations are spending billions on training staff and managers (£14 billion in 1986–7 in the UK alone [Pell, 1989]).

The industry in which I am involved, banking, is a typical example. Changes in competition, technology and products necessitate training on a vast scale. The economy is no longer at the bottom of a trough, and governments, for example in the European Community, are actively encouraging training initiatives.

Three years ago I was in discussion with the training manager of a prominent UK company about introducing evaluation into his training interventions. 'I don't believe in evaluation!' he told me, 'I have built up a reputation in the company for providing good training programmes; I don't need evaluation while the board has faith in what I am doing.' I spoke to him a month later: 'They've cut my training budget by over one third!' I tried to contact him again after that; he had gone sick for the forseeable future.

The point is that training and development may be tolerated by the company as an act of faith at certain times – usually when money is available and when there is an immediately perceived need, such as in periods of technological change and in preparing employees for new jobs. In business terms, expenditure on training and development is an investment in human resources. In accounting terms, however, it is not usually seen as that, and is regarded as an expense: it does not give a tangible return. The battle to persuade the accountancy profession to adopt the principles of human resource accounting was fought some years ago (see Flamholtz, 1974), and I do not intend to re-fight that battle within these pages. However, a company still needs to see a return on its investment. Far from training being a luxury unrelated to the business needs of an organization, it is integral to business success. If it is able to contribute to business objectives, then it is capable of yielding a return for the organization.

Evaluating human resource programmes is not new. It can be traced back to at least the 1940s when Brogden (1949) published a paper on the original concept of 'utility analysis' which gained some acceptance in the United States and has since been developed by advocates such as Cascio (1982). Utility analysis has never really gained acceptance in the UK for it can be complicated, needing sophisticated statistical computations. In fact, evaluation in the human resource development field has never really caught on at all in Britain, and has still a long way to go in the United States. Many publications seem to skirt round the subject of the value of training and development and miss the real point, which is as follows. Evaluation is about the 'value' of training to an organization. Value in business terms is described in pounds, dollars or other currency. If value cannot be demonstrated in these terms, there may still be a benefit to the individual or the organization, but this probably is not realizable in business terms.

This book will help you – novice or experienced trainer, training manager, personnel specialist or consultant – to place your training and development programmes in the context of evaluation by making them results-orientated and capable of yielding demonstrable bottom-line benefits to your organization. Although the book is mainly directed towards commercial organizations, there is increasing pressure on public sector organizations, such as local authorities and health authorities, to be more cost-effective in their use of resources, and much of what is said in this text will also be relevant to that environment.

Terence Jackson

Part 1
Introduction

1. Evaluation in context

The trainer as business man or woman

Evaluation in human resource development is not an activity which can be 'bolted on' to a training or development course. It is a fundamental approach to training and development which sees trainers, or managers of training, as business persons who have a definite contribution to make to business results. Trainers do not necessarily see themselves in this light.

Personnel departments in general, and training and development in particular, have tended to be the poor relations. The attitude of the boardroom has been, 'If we can afford them we will have them; if not, we can do without!' Unfortunately, this has been the fault of the trainers themselves. They are reluctant to tie in their performance with the performance of the business. They have been reluctant, or unable, to show the contribution of their efforts to profits. They have said this cannot be done; that measures of performance, especially in an office environment and particularly in management training, are too subjective to be able to attach a cash benefit to them. They have been frightened to do it. Suppose the training function does *not* contribute to profits!

There is a whole number of reasons why trainers should not evaluate their efforts, but only if training and development is seen as a separate issue and unrelated to the business which organizations are in. If training and development is seen as integral to the organization's business, then evaluation ceases to be an issue and becomes a fact of life.

To clarify some of these points, it is worth returning to basics at this stage, defining some terms, and reminding ourselves what training and development is all about.

Business management: The role of management is to ensure that resources are used in the most efficient and effective way. In other words, the job of a manager is to provide a service in the most cost- and resource-efficient way possible, and to provide the best possible service with the resources available. That is, to provide for the organization the maximum return on the capital employed in the business.

Let us define some widely used terms more precisely.

Efficiency: providing the same service with less outlay or resources (cost savings).

Effectiveness: providing a better service with the same outlay or resources (increased benefits).

Productivity: providing a better service with less outlay or resources (cost savings and increased benefits).

How well a company, or part of a company, performs in these terms is measurable. Typical measures are:

$$\text{Profits per employee} = \frac{\text{Trading profits}}{\text{Number of employees}}$$

$$\text{Output per employee} = \frac{\text{Units produced or processed}}{\text{Number of employees}}$$

$$\text{Value added per employee} = \frac{\text{Value added (sales revenue} - \text{cost of sales)}}{\text{Number of employee}}$$

In each ratio, the numerator is an indication of effectiveness, whereas the denominator indicates efficiency. Productivity can be changed by altering either or both of these. For example, a department may become more effective by increasing the number of units produced while retaining the same number of employees. Alternatively, it may become more efficient by reducing its number of staff but maintaining output at the same level.

To see what relevance this has to training and development, let us now define these two terms. *Training* (noun) is a set of management tools with the function of improving an organization's current performance in terms of efficiency, effectiveness and productivity. The tools are used to develop skills and knowledge as a means of increasing individual, operational and organizational performance. *Development* (noun) is also a set of management tools, but the investment is mainly made for the future performance of the organization, and is connected to organizational objectives for the future. The tools are used to enhance the skills and abilities which the individual needs to be able to move with the organization and to pursue a career in line with its evolving needs.

As a bag of management tools there is nothing which sets training and development apart from the other tools, techniques or methods which the manager has available. Its usefulness to the manager can only be defined by the results it helps the manager achieve. If training and development does not contribute to achieving the required results, more emphasis can be placed on other tools, techniques or methods. These other tools should be known to the trainer as alternatives to those of training and development. The trainer should not necessarily be an expert in the use of these other tools, but should know when they are more appropriate than training and development, or when they can be used together with training and development.

A trainer is not simply a person who stands up in front of a class and teaches skills or knowledge. This is an instructor, presenter, teacher, lecturer, tutor or group facilitator: terms which reflect methods of classroom delivery. A trainer is someone who has responsibility to line management for the use of a set of tools and techniques aimed at developing skills and knowledge to improve the performance of individuals, groups and the organization. It is not ultimately the responsibility of the trainer to make sure that skills learned off the job are applied on the job and that they affect operational performance. This is the responsibility of the line manager. The line manager delegates the responsibility of training to a trainer, to a subordinate on the job, or does it him or herself. In either case the line manager is responsible for the operational performance of his or her section or department. Trainers are responsible for their own performance, however, and this is determined by their ability successfully to identify the business needs of the organization, the operational needs of the line managers and the skills and knowledge requirements of individuals in their jobs. It is also determined by their ability successfully to develop appropriate skills and knowledge in individuals, and to gain the commitment and involvement of both trainees and their line managers in applying those skills and knowledge in the workplace. The success of the trainer in identifying needs and developing appropriate skills can only be determined by evidence of results in the workplace, and evidence of the contribution of these operational results to business or organizational success.

Business results are typically measured in financial terms. This is the currency of the business man or woman. This is the currency of the trainer.

Evaluation as a results-orientated approach to training and development

If training and development has *value* for the organization it can be *evaluated*. For training and development to have this value, trainers must make sure that it is directed towards the business objectives of the organization. This business orientation is taken up in some detail later, particularly in Chapters 2 and 3. Here we focus on the 'tools' of training, both as a process and within a training and development 'system'. By first focusing on the process of training and development it is possible to see how the basic 'tools' may be used to direct training to a results orientation. This training focus is of course the preoccupation of trainers; businesses, however, focus on the business process which produces results. If training provides results within this process, it is useful; if not, other management tools and methods will be used to enhance results.

Although the rest of this book focuses on the business process and how training and development fits into this, this particular section of the text focuses on and outlines the process of results-orientated training and development, and looks at the tools available in the trainer's bag. A useful model for doing this is seen in Figure 1.1.

Identification of training needs

Line managers may feel that there is a training need because current staff performance could be improved. There may be an increase in work, and therefore a need to process more with the same staff. Systems changes and changes in the technology employed may result in redundant knowledge and skills and a perceived need to train staff in the new skills and knowledge. An influx of new staff may also result in a need for training. In all these cases, management may call on the services of the training function within an organization. In this respect, training is a *reactive* function and responds to calls by the line to investigate training needs and to deliver appropriate training.

There is another way of viewing training, and this is particularly apparent in periods of organizational change where there is a need for trainers to become involved in operational planning: to advise on what is possible in terms of the skills potential of the workforce, and on how much change should be implemented at any one time. Although this may not operate in practice where the training function is not seen as part of the business process, if the situation arises it is an opportunity for trainers to take a more *proactive* role in the organization. On the whole, however, training and development is a reactive function, responding to the demands of the line.

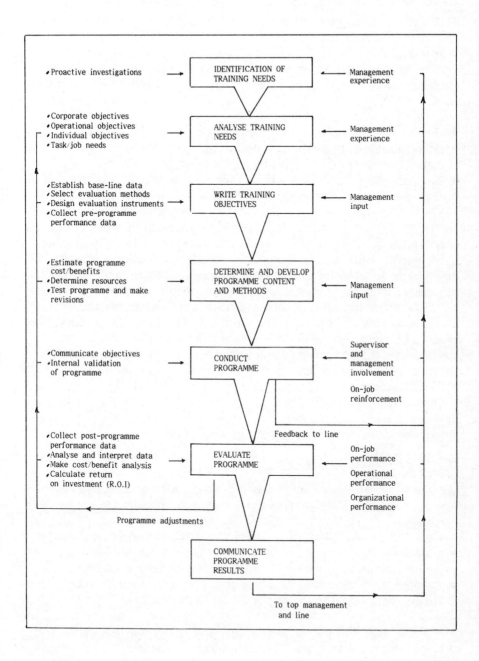

Figure 1.1 Results-orientated training model

Analysis of training needs

This is the first professional input of the trainer, although it relies on the experience of line management to correctly reflect the needs of the organization.

A training-needs analysis is conducted to determine whether training is needed and, if so, what training. Training is needed if two conditions exist:

- there is a gap between the actual performance and the required performance of individuals, operational units, and the organization, either currently or in the future
- the gap can be closed by developing skills and knowledge which increase the performance of individuals and groups.

A training-needs analysis should begin with an understanding of corporate objectives, of what needs to be done operationally to achieve corporate objectives, and of what skills and knowledge are required by individuals to achieve operational objectives. Skills and knowledge requirements are determined by specifying the key results areas of each job, the tasks undertaken to achieve results in these areas, and the type and level of skills and knowledge required to perform these tasks. This aspect of training is discussed in some detail later (Chapter 2), as it is a key to evaluating training and development interventions. It is at this stage in the training process that the criteria for evaluation are laid down by determining the current level of performance against the desired level of performance. Evaluation measures success in closing the gap between these two, and the extent to which training and development helps meet operational and corporate objectives.

Writing training objectives

On the basis of a training-needs analysis, training objectives can be written. Objectives should specify:

- the skills and knowledge to be developed for key functions of the job
- how skills applied in the job should impact on job performance
- how this skills application should affect operational results
- how the expected operational results will impact organizationally and in line with corporate objectives.

This is the ideal! The following chapters will help you to reach this ideal.

It is at this stage that base-line data should be established, evaluation methods should be selected, evaluation instruments should be designed, and pre-training performance data collected. Consider Figure 1.2.

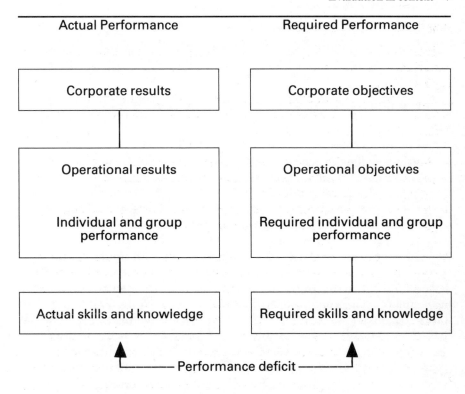

Figure 1.2 The performance gap

Required performance is governed by: the objectives set down by the policy makers of the organization; those operational results needed to meet corporate objectives; those individual and group performances needed to achieve operational results; and the skills and knowledge necessary for the individual to perform to requirements.

To determine whether, as a result of training, the performance deficit has decreased, actual performance should be measured or assessed at this pre-training stage (the difference between 'assessment' and 'measurement' is discussed in Chapter 4). After training, performance can again be measured to determine the difference. What is measured and how it is measured can only be determined by the nature of the job, and the way performance, operational results and corporate results are currently measured. This will then indicate the methods and specific instruments to be used in the assessment and measurement of results. These will be examined in Chapter 4.

Whatever methods and measures are used, the involvement and commitment of line and senior management must be obtained at this stage. In fact, it is impossible to get this far without management driving this effort. You, the trainer, are simply providing the expertise to get the vehicle on the road, to navigate the course, and to maintain the mechanics of the vehicle. This book will help you to design the vehicle.

Determining and developing programme content and methods

The next stage is to establish the content of the training programme based on objectives and the method of its delivery. This book will tell you little specifically about programme design; rather, it will tell you how to estimate the benefits as well as determine the costs of alternative programme designs. You have already incurred an expense, if only by using your own time, in performing the preliminary work described above. This must all be added into the cost of training.

Calculating the cost of training only shows one side of the equation, and shows it only as an expense not an investment. By estimating the potential benefits of training programmes, the expense can be justified. This would normally be undertaken by reference to the close in the performance gap which is anticipated as a result of training. Chapter 6 looks specifically at cost-benefit analysis. Other management methods may be applicable to the problem, and your estimates, which can be calculated with line management involved, will help the line make a decision about different training methods and alternative management tools.

At this stage the training design can be piloted, and, after measuring the performance of participants in the job, it can be revised as necessary.

Conducting the programme

Before conducting the programme, the objectives of the training should be communicated to the line, although in cases where the programme is offered to a restricted group the line would already have had maximum involvement in formulating course objectives. It is particularly important that the programme participants' immediate supervisors are fully involved, otherwise the training may fail to have impact in the job. The supervisor should have mentoring and coaching skills where possible, so that the programme participant can be supported and guided in the application of skills in the workplace.

Training is doomed to failure if this level of support is not gained from the line. It is ultimately a line responsibility to ensure that subordinates are trained in accordance with organizational requirement!

Good communication back to the line is essential. Evaluation provides management information on the effectivenesss of training and development as management tools. Although this information is important at all stages of the training process, as we will see later, it begins to take on an added importance at this point, where the line is contributing to the success or failure of training.

Evaluating the programme

Data should be gathered at all levels, as indicated in Figure 1.2 above. The timing of collecting this data depends on the nature of the job, the operation and the objectives and nature of the training programme. Analysis and interpretation of data depends on the methods used and the nature of the data. Obviously data collected and analysed at this stage should be directly comparable to data collected and analysed before the training programme.

A question arises at this stage. How do we know that it is the training that has affected our data and not any other factors impacting on performance? This question will be taken up in more detail later in the book (Chapter 3). Any solution must be given consideration when training objectives are written.

The two most common solutions to this problem are either to use a 'control group' which does not receive the training as a means of comparison, or to use a 'time series' design to detect other factors impacting on the group being trained. These are illustrated in Figure 1.3.

Control group method

Group 1

Measure performance – – – – → Train – – – – → Measure performance

Group 2 (control)

Measure performance – – – – – – – – – – – – → Measure performance

Time Series Method

Measure performance	Measure performance		Measure performance	Measure performance
1	2	Train – →	3	4

Figure 1.3 Designs for isolating other factors impacing on performance

The only problems with these designs is that they can be impractical in a fast-moving company environment where training needs to take place quickly or needs to include everyone as soon as possible. Alternatives will be discussed later (Chapter 3).

Post-programme performance data should be compared with pre-programme data, and the close in the performance deficit measured. This should be done at individual performance level, operational level, and ultimately at corporate level. The close in the performance deficit indicates the benefits of the programme to the organization and can be stated in financial terms. Benefits should be compared to the cost of training to see whether the cost was justified, to see if training as a management tool was appropriate in this case, and to provide an indication to senior management that the training budget is being well spent and providing a return on investment for the organization. This almost completes the process, but not quite.

Communicating programme results

One of the biggest benefits to the organization to be derived from an evaluation strategy is the provision of management information, as we have previously stated. This does not just apply to training and development. It applies to the evaluation of any management tool where resources have been allocated.

Information on results should be communicated to top management. It should also be fed back into the process via line management. This tells the line whether the performance gap has been decreased, and if there remains a further need to use either training or other management tools to increase performance in line with corporate and operational objectives. It shows whether business objectives are indeed being met.

Meeting business objectives: a basic model for evaluation

We have focused on the training process and on how evaluation fits into this. Let us now look at training and development in its appropriate position within the *business* process: as a set of management tools, its use directed at attaining business objectives. In doing so we will construct a basic model which can be used as a template for evaluation design. This model is further developed in Chapters 2 and 3.

Training and development, as a set of management tools, should improve skills and knowledge in such a way as to affect current performance (training) or future performance (development) in the job. This is measurable by noting changes in behaviour. These changes in behaviour should impact on operational results. Operational results are measured in terms of inputs and outputs. Inputs are resources such as money and staff. Outputs are typically units sold, items produced or tasks completed. Inputs are measurable in terms of time (for example staff hours employed) and costs (for example unit costs). Outputs are measured in volume processed and quality of work (for example scrap or error rates).

Operational results can therefore be shown by a ratio of outputs per inputs (for example tasks completed per staff hour employed). Operational results should then impact on corporate objectives. Results at the corporate level are measured in financial terms: profits or return on assets, for example. The value of training and development is therefore financial: if it does not contribute to corporate (financial) objectives it is not of value as a management tool and other management tools may be appropriate. The model is shown in Figure 1.4.

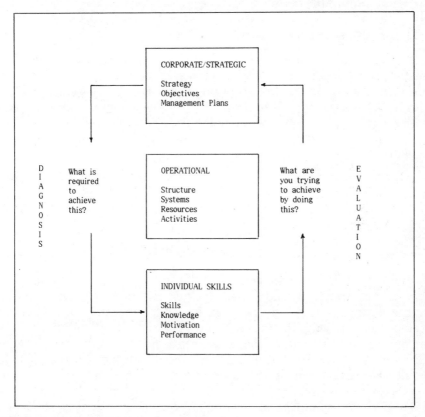

Figure 1.4 A model for evaluation design

The diagnostic phase

Remembering that training and development is only one set of tools available to the management team, any use of these tools must be set in the context of the total management effort.

The first questions to be asked, therefore, are: What is the direction of this management effort? What are the corporate objectives?

Second, to achieve these key corporate objectives, what needs to be done operationally? This might be in terms of organizational structure, systems, resources or activities.

Thirdly, to achieve operational results with the structure, systems, resources and activities needed or employed, what skills and knowledge need to be developed?

This completes a diagnostic phase which should conclude with the production of appropriate training objectives and a training product (assuming that other management tools are not more appropriate where there is a limit to the financial resources available).

The evaluation process

If training objectives are now in line with corporate objectives following the diagnostic phase, the evaluation phase can be undertaken.

First, what skills and/or knowledge are assessable as a result of training? Criteria should be developed so that it can be known when skills have been learned and applied in the job. For example:

Skill	*Criteria*
Making decisions	Improved timeliness and quality of decisions made, to save time and costs and reduce errors/improve quality
Team working	Better cooperation, to obtain results more quickly and of better quality.

Second, what is line management trying to achieve operationally by developing these skills and knowledge? Operational objectives should be stated, together with the way results can be measured and what the results are, following the training intervention. All operational results are measurable, no matter what work is processed. If staff do something different as a result of training, this should impact on measurable results. However, they are sometimes difficult to measure directly, and indirect methods of assessment are looked at in Chapter 4 and 5.

Thirdly, by achieving operational objectives, what strategic or corporate results are senior management trying to achieve? The targets should be stated and the actual results achieved should be demonstrable.

At each stage (individual skills, operational and corporate/strategic) other factors may impact on overall results. These factors should be identified, isolated and possible effects determined. This, in outline, is an evaluation process which will ensure that training is in line with corporate objectives and will produce results which can be communicated in financial terms to the board of directors or policy makers of the organization. From this basic model we will develop a template which can be used to evaluate training and development in your organization.

Part 2
Evaluation Strategy

2. The diagnostic process

Training for bottom-line results

Evaluation, as we have already discussed, is not an add-on feature to training and development; it is an integral part of the process of training and development. The diagnostic part of this process ensures that training is directed towards bottom-line results.

It is no good simply evaluating training. This leaves to chance the results of this evaluation. It might turn out that the training you are doing is of no value to the organization. So why not stack the cards in your favour, to make sure that any training undertaken is orientated towards achieving bottom-line results?

This chapter provides a template for doing that. It is based on the model in Figure 1.4 and it covers three levels of diagnosis:

- corporate objectives
- operational needs and objectives
- skill requirements.

The template is shown in Figure 2.1.

By the end of this chapter you should know how to use this template. This should help you to design training and development programmes which are orientated towards bottom-line results.

Corporate objectives

You need first to find out what the key corporate objectives of your organization are. The difficulty or ease of your obtaining this information will depend on:

- whether or not your organization has clear corporate objectives
- how well published or publicized these objectives are

CORPORATE REQUIREMENTS/OBJECTIVES

What are the key objectives?   Targets?

1. . . . .
2. . . . .
3. . . . .
4. . . . .
5. . . . .

OPERATIONAL NEEDS/OBJECTIVES

To achieve corporate objectives:

	What is being done at operational level?	What needs to be done at operational level?
Structure	. . . .	. . . .
Systems	. . . .	. . . .
Resources	. . . .	. . . .
Activities	. . . .	. . . .

SKILLS REQUIREMENTS

What skills need to be developed to achieve operational results?

Skills	. . . . : . . . .
Knowledge	. . . .
Motivation	. . . .
Performance (Outcome)	. . . .

Figure 2.1. Template for diagnosis

- if they are not readily available, your relative position and seniority in the organization
- your ability to obtain the relevant information
- your skill in interpreting this information to extract that which is important and relevant.

Corporate plans are statements of direction and goals, and of how such goals might be achieved. Corporate planning is the art of the possible, of taking into consideration the capabilities of the organization within the realities of its environment. Not all organizations have corporate plans. Without having objectives, explicit or otherwise, it is very easy for an organization to stagnate or take a wrong turn. Many companies have implicit (or even covert) objectives, but these are more difficult to extract from the policy makers.

Within large organizations the various divisions, departments or subsidiaries may have their own management objectives which should be in line with the overall corporate objectives. Often, corporate plans are hierarchial in nature (see for example Armstrong, 1986) and if the organization is divided functionally (for example into buying, production, selling, accounting etc) then the various parts of the organization may have objectives which reflect this hierarchy. This is illustrated in Figure 2.2.

Also reflecting this hierarchial make-up is the way in which corporate objectives can be defined, in terms of:

- the organization's mission
- goals and strategies
- objectives and tactics
- policies, procedures and rules
  (Gannon, 1982).

A *mission statement* results from a clear understanding of the environment in which the organization is working and the way that environment is changing. It is a definition of what market the company is in, in terms of the range of services and the clientele it serves. For example, building societies in the UK have traditionally provided finance for home purchase. After looking at the markets they are actually in – house buying and finance – many now offer a full range of services for the house-buyer, including estate agency and (pending legal changes) conveyancing, and a full range of personal financial services in competition with the banks. Long-term *goals* are then formulated. This may involve stating the market share which the company hopes to achieve in each market segment over the next five years. The means to achieve such goals are the *strategies* adopted. For example, after setting a goal of achieving 10 per cent of the mortgage market, a bank might

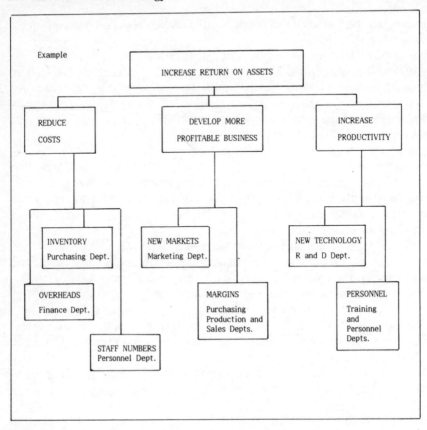

Figure 2.2. Hierarchy of objectives by function

develop a plan of action to develop certain mortgage products which will compete with building societies and other banks. *Objectives* are usually short-term goals, often expressed over a 12-month period. They are usually directed towards the longer-term goals of the organization. For example, having decided to capture a 10 per cent share of the market in mortgages over the next five years, a bank might set an objective for the year to increase home loan sales by 15 per cent.

It might be wise at this stage to consider the difference between goals, objectives and *targets*. A goal is an expression of a long-term aim with some indication of how it is known that the aim has been achieved. Similarly, an objective is a short-term aim with some expression of how it is known that it has been arrived at. A target is such an expression; it demonstrates success (or otherwise) in achieving what has been set out to be achieved. An objective, for example, might be 'to increase sales'. The degree of success in doing this is only demonstrable by stating a specific target – for example 'to increase sales by 15 per cent by the end of the year'. Targets are the criteria against which performance can be measured.

Tactics are those actions taken to achieve these short-term objectives, and therefore a company or organization's long-term goals. For example, a bank might introduce a low-start mortgage to attract more customers. *Policies, procedures and rules* are directions laid down by top management to direct day-to-day activities towards objectives and goals. They are guides to action and act as controls on the work of the organization; they extend from the general (policies) to the specific (rules).

There can be problems with corporate goals and objectives. Corporate goals are not corporate goals, they are 'executive' goals (see for example Katz and Kahn, 1978, who query in what sense organizations have goals). As goals and objectives are laid down by the top of the organization, individuals on other levels might not know about them, if they are not properly communicated, those individuals might not agree with or share them.

The problems which the trainer may encounter are as follows:

- there are no obvious corporate goals
- there are corporate goals but they are not communicated downwards
- corporate goals are communicated downwards, but operational and individual activities are at variance with them.

What can the trainer do to identify key corporate objectives and targets which have implications for operational objectives and actions, and consequently have implications for the skills required to achieve objectives? The following may be helpful.

1. Interview the chief executive or head of a major operating unit. This may produce a handful of objectives, but may not necessarily produce specific targets. There may be things the chief executive does not want to disclose about a particular direction because it may, for example, have implications for trade union relations if it were publicly known.

The top management of your organization may not work on the basis of setting objectives. However, commercial organizations do not last very long in a competitive market-place without clearly defined objectives! You may like to suggest developing a course on strategic thinking at this stage. If you are an internal trainer it may be necessary to use an outside consultant to obtain politically sensitive information which would not normally be available to an 'insider'.

At this stage it is essential that you get the support, if not the clear direction, of top management if you are to progress. Explain what you are trying to do, the benefits to the organization and the information you need to achieve it.

2. Study public documents such as the company's annual report, and other documents such as management plans where these are available. These provide written statements of where the organization, or parts of it, should be going. If there is a management by objectives (MBO) scheme in your organization, where objectives set by managers are in line with corporate objectives, your task will be that much easier.

3. Try to trace back from actions taking place in the organization to strategic decisions taken. What is going on in your organization? Just because top management has not made public its corporate plans, this does not mean that you do not know what is going on around you!

Is there a new computer system being planned? Ask why. See if you can find out the thinking behind this and why it is being planned. Is it to improve performance in a certain area? Is it to project a new image to the customer? Armstrong (1986) suggests that strategic plans tend to involve the following areas:

- marketing
- organizational growth
- technological innovation
- cost reduction
- productivity
- finance.

You can probably see what is happening in the first five areas, but you may not be privy to financial objectives. In this last category specific targets are set in financial terms; for example, what profits are needed over the coming period to finance company growth. These targets result from meeting specific objectives in the other five areas.

Find out specific targets if possible, although this is not absolutely essential at this stage. More will be said on corporate objectives when we look at the evaluation phase in Chapter 3. Your main task is to ascertain the *implications* of corporate objectives. What is required to achieve corporate objectives? What is actually being done to achieve corporate objectives? We address these questions in the following section.

To conclude, we have stated the problems of identifying corporate objectives. These are many, but it remains the task of the trainer to at least identify those key corporate objectives which may have the greatest impact on organizational life: operational actions and skill requirements. This will begin to ensure that existing training that is being undertaken or investigated is in line with corporate requirements, is up to date, and is in line with the changing needs of the organization.

Once the key objectives have been identified (refer above for the differences between mission, goals and objectives), specific targets should be ascertained where possible. In a large organization this may have to be done for each department. In this case, the hierarchical nature of corporate objectives and how this extends downwards to particular functional parts of the organization (for example departments and divisions should be remembered).

This is an excellent time to explain your evaluation strategy to, and gain the commitment of, the chief executive. It is at this point that you need to *sell* evaluation. This is taken up in Chapter 6.

Operational needs and objectives

We have started off the diagnostic phase by looking at corporate objectives. This was not from the position of strategic analysis, as we are not so much interested in the rightness or wrongness of particular corporate objectives, but in the implications they have for what goes on at the operational level. As trainers, this is the level at which we begin to get involved.

Although it is possible to get involved in skills training at any of these levels – for example, it may be necessary to propose input at the corporate/strategic level where the required strategic skills are not being displayed by top management (although tread carefully with this proposal!) – our main input will probably start with line managers, and will directly impact on operational performance.

We should therefore look at:

- the implications of corporate strategy and tactics, for operational objectives
- the operational factors in which trainers are interested – namely structure, systems, resources and activities.

Strategies and tactics turn corporate goals and objectives into reality, as we have seen (page 21). To do this, the way the organization works needs to be planned and adapted. The way the organization is structured; the systems which operate within it to throughput information, process work or distribute goods; the resources of materials, space, people and time; and the activities in which people within the organization participate, all need to be planned in a way that ensures corporate objectives and goals are achieved. There should be a direct link between what is being done operationally and corporate objectives. Line managers may have their own section's or department's objectives which are directed towards the achievement of corporate objectives.

Is this the case in your organization? Can you answer the question,

'What is being done operationally to achieve corporate objectives?' Let us see what you should be looking for.

Structure

As trainers we are interested in people. People work within an organizational structure. This structure may be such that it facilitates work or hampers it; it may facilitate or hinder the achievement of business objectives. The formal structure may be circumvented or subverted. It is unlikely that it is adhered to strictly, but some structures may be more flexible than others and may allow for, or even encourage, innovation while controlling the degree of risk involved in innovation.

The structure of an organization may have come about in response to events, or may be strategically driven to address specific corporate objectives. Structure is the way lines of authority, decision making and communication are drawn. Structure affects people's activities and attitudes. The more formal the structure, where vertical lines of authority and decision making are strictly adhered to, the less commitment staff will have the further they are away from the decision maker (see Leavitt, 1951, for one of the classic studies on this, which still holds true). This does not bode well for the pursuit of corporate objectives!

You may like to note in your organization where the purpose of actions in relation to corporate objectives starts to get a bit unclear. This may be a result of the structure. Changing the structure of an organization is usually an action which is strategic in nature and included in long-term goals. Structure has implications for requirements at the skills level.

Consider the following types of structure listed by Greiner and Metzger (1983):

- A *functional* structure divides the organization into units performing a particular specialism, such as buying, production or marketing.
- A *product* structure is market-driven, with each unit serving a particular type of customer.
- A *geographic* structure serves customers in different geographical locations
- A *project* structure addresses specific one-off projects which although one-off are within the nature of the business undertaken.
- A *matrix* organization combines a functional structure with a project structure, where there is a need to draw project teams from various functional units.

These different structures have different skills requirements. A functional structure has a need for specialization to a higher degree than a product or geographical structure where functional units may be smaller and have a need for a wider range of skills in the individual. Project structures may require the particular skills of project management. A product structure will require a strong marketing focus, particularly in a service industry, and perhaps additional skills in this area.

Greiner and Metzger (1983) also suggest particular issues which are prominent in decisions regarding structural changes. These are as follows.

Decentralization: attempting to push decision making downwards so the organization is more responsive to local or market events and needs.

Centralization: placing tighter control over diverse organizational units to provide better coordination and effective deployment of resources.

Regrouping: attempting to stem and recoordinate *ad hoc* growth in an organization to improve coordination and market response.

Coordination: providing greater coordination between functioning units to better respond to the changing needs of the marketplace.

Job analysis: rationalizing the organization of jobs, particularly in a situation of technological change where existing jobs and methods of organizing job families may quickly become redundant.

Information and control: altering the structure to provide management information more effectively, giving a greater degree of control. This is really an assessment of information needs in line with corporate objectives and increased business efficiency generally, and in line with the introduction of new systems.

Tactical planning: the structure may have to alter in line with tactical planning, but in order to facilitate such planning certain forms of structure may work better. An example is where planning may need to come from the bottom up or sideways across departments, such as in the case of marketing department planning giving the impetus for production planning.

We can add a further consideration to these issues: employee motivation and work satisfaction.

Employee motivation and work satisfaction: by giving individual staff more responsibility and a wider collection of tasks, job satisfaction may increase. This has implications for structure at the bottom end of the organization, such as implementation of the 'Volvo' principle, allowing a wider range of tasks to be undertaken by individuals within a work group.

Again these issues, put into effect, raise certain training implications. What are the issues involved in structural decisions in your organization and what are their implications for training? For example, restructuring in response to task redundancy when introducing new computer systems requires learning new skills with obvious training implications. Similarly, when job clusters are regrouped, requiring a wider range of skills for a job, additional training is required.

Systems

By 'systems' we mean the way in which inputs to the organization, or specific parts of the organization, are processed (throughputted) and outputted. Topically this has meant information systems and that is the emphasis here, although it is not exclusively the case. There are production systems, for example, which govern the throughput of work in the organization, but this is usually placed under the heading of 'structure' (the way organizations are structured functionally to provide a throughput of work) or resources (the physical resources used for processing the work).

The implications of computer information systems to the training needs of an organization include the following:

- The supply and type of information available within the organization has implications for what staff and managers need to know and what they need to be able to do with the information.
- Management action may be different as a result of the type of information available. This may have a 'knock-on' effect on jobs further down the line, as well as on the jobs of the managers.
- Contacts between individuals in the organization may change as a result of the way information flows through the organization. Wider contacts may lead to a requirement for wider skills and knowledge. Narrower contacts may lead to a narrower or different skills requirement.
- User attitudes and perceptions may alter both the way people work and their productivity. This may be something that can be addressed by training.
- The technical quality of the system may have implications for the way the system is used, attitudes towards it and skills needed to use it.
- The nature of the system has implications for the skills and knowledge required to use it.
- The physical location and situation of the user may have implications for the way the user works and therefore the skills required.

- The different nature of the work involved may require different types of decisions to be made by the user. This may have training implications.

(See for example Lucas, 1985)

What are the implications for training of information systems within your organization, or for planned systems within your organization?

Resources

Resources within an organization include the following:

- premises and actual working space
- machinery, equipment and tools
- raw materials
- stock-in-trade
- consumables
- money
- people
- time
- information.

These are organized within a particular structure and relate to each other in terms of structure, systems and activities in such a way that they meet the particular purposes or functions of the organization.

Resources employed have implications for training requirements in the following ways:

- The type of machinery, equipment and tools employed require particular skills to use them.
- The resources 'consumed' in the work process (either raw materials or actual consumables such as stationery) require the use of particular skills and knowledge.
- Money available determines the availability of other resources in the organization. The scarcity or availability of equipment, people and time has an effect on the degree of skills and types of skills required.
- The type of information and systems used for conveying and processing that information has implications for the skills and knowledge required.
- The people brought into the organization, their abilities, skills and knowledge, have a major impact on the training required within the organization.

What are the skills and training implications of the resources currently available in your organization for current needs and for the needs of the next five-year period over which time the present corporate goals are going to be pursued?

Activities

The formal *current* activities within an organization (that is, the activities which are directed towards pursuing the purposes and functions of the organization) are largely determined by the following factors:

- the purpose for which the organization exists
- the implementation of strategic and tactical plans directed towards specific corporate (executive) goals and objectives
- *ad hoc* decisions made by management in response to day-to-day events or changes in the organization or the marketplace
- specific objectives (explicit or implicit) of the individuals who make up the organization, their attitudes and motivations
- the structure of the organization
- information and other processing systems in the organization
- the resources within the organization
- the design of actual jobs and tasks within the organization
- actual skills, knowledge and motivation of job holders related specifically to the particular jobs currently held

The *potential* activities which the organization could undertake if they were in line with future plans and not currently undertaken, depend on the *capability* of the organization, specifically:

- the current or potential financial resources
- the current or potential skills, knowledge, abilities and attitudes of current human resources
- the potential of the marketplace or environment within which the organization works
- the capabilities for development of the organizational structure and systems
- the availability of resources.

All these factors have a bearing on the training required within the organization. This is directly related to the activities undertaken which can be classified in terms of:

Level of analysis	*Activities of:*
Job family	eg Accounts and Budgets Officers
Occupation/job type	eg Budgets Officer, Accounts Officer

Level of analysis	*Activities of:*
Job	eg Budgets Officer 1 in Company A, Budgets Officer 1 in Company B
Position	eg Person 1 in Company A who performs tasks 1, 2, and 3
Task	eg Producing cash-flow analysis
Behaviour	eg making entry in ledger, adding up figures in ledger

(See for example Pearlman, 1980)

We have therefore seen that the operational arrangements of an organization and its objectives affect the skills required. In the next section we look more specifically at operational requirements and results, and their implications for skills requirements and the provision of training.

Skills requirements

The term 'skills' has been used here to include:

- skills
- knowledge
- motivation
- performance.

Why it has been used in this context may be better explained by referring to Argyle's (1967) skills model in Figure 2.3.

This is seen as a conscious process directed towards making changes in our environment. It requires some sort of motivation. It also requires an ability to perceive the changes to be made; to understand how they can be achieved; to apply this understanding to the perceived situation; and to formulate the action. Finally, we can monitor the actual changes we make and compare them with our intentions. Through our ability to perceive what we are doing, we can then make suitable adjustments to our behaviour to ensure the desired result is achieved.

These factors are all part of a 'skilled performance' requiring:

- motivation to perform
- knowledge of what is required
- the ability to translate knowledge into specific behaviour
- the performance itself which provides evidence that the above three factors are present.

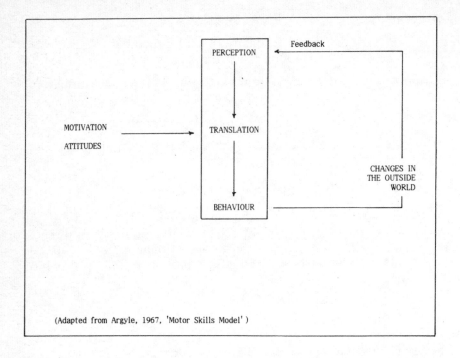

(Adapted from Argyle, 1967, 'Motor Skills Model')

Figure 2.3 Argyle's skills model

Skills can be defined as:

> . . .the capability to perform job operations with ease and precision.
> (Prien E, quoted in Goldstein, 1986)

This implies some sort of value judgement as to the standard of work produced. These standards are usually laid down by the organization through the policies, procedures and rules we discussed earlier (page 21), as well as by accepted practices for particular industries, trades and professions, by government legislation or other external regulatory controls.

We are particularly interested here in the outcome (or required outcome) of skilled performances, when this is affected by the *policies, procedures and rules* laid down in the organization as a consequence of strategic planning: where standards of work are laid down so that operational and corporate objectives may be met. Standards may relate to the quantity of work and the quality of work. An example of quality follows.

The banks and other financial companies are in an increasingly competitive situation, where products are very similar between institutions. With strategic objectives set at increasing market penetration, the main distinguishing factor between institutions is the quality of service offered to customers. If a bank continually provides a bad service through paying cancelled standing orders, long queues in the banking hall, or cash machines out of order, the customer is going to move accounts. The high street banks are therefore paying particular attention to the quality of their customer service, laying down policies from the top of the organization and deriving procedures, rules and standards of service from the bottom of the organization.

Standards are judged by criteria laid down for the results of a skilled performance, rather than the process itself. Criteria do not usually relate to the motivation required to get the job done, nor to the perception and translation processes. Sometimes criteria relate to the behaviour required, but mostly to the changes made in the environment: the quantity and quality of the work produced or processed. The problem for the trainer in the organization is that quite often standards of performance do not exist in an explicit form for all or any of the jobs in the organization. If this is the case what can you do to find out:

- what standards are required by the organization to ensure corporate objectives are met?
- what is the shortfall in actual performance compared with standards required for current performance?
- what is the shortfall in actual current performance compared with standards for performance required in the future to meet objectives?

There are various ways you can look at this. First, you can look at the norms of the work group where people are performing similar jobs, or the norms of the particular job group across the industry. Practical methods of doing this are discussed in Part 3 (Evaluation Methods). Secondly, you can derive standards from the requirements of operational objectives and targets. If a particular operational objective is set for increasing the quality of customer service, this objective is impossible to achieve unless standards are agreed. Ask line managers and staff the following question:

'How do you know when you are providing a quality service to customers?'

You might get some of the following answers:

- no customer complaints
- waiting time for customers down to a few minutes
- customers' queries settled first time, no follow up, no referrals to supervisor

- referral of new customers from existing customers
- minimum closure of existing accounts.

It is possible to measure some of these exactly. For example: the number of complaints per number of customers; the number of account closures per number of account holders; the number of new accounts as a result of referrals by existing customers. From this, specific targets can be set. For example, complaints down to 2 per cent of customers; account closures down to 1 per cent of accounts held.

Standards will be based on the targets set, as these are the operational requirements of the organization. If these standards, derived from operational needs, are required in current performance, one of two conditions will exist. Either, the standards are currently being met, or the standards are not currently being met.

The next set of questions to ask, if standards are not being met, is: Why are standards not being achieved? What is required to enable them to be met? These questions lead us back to the 'performance deficit' portrayed in Figure 1.2, and the major issue in training as a management tool: *if there is a skills performance gap between what is and what should be, then training is probably an appropriate management tool to use.* In other words, we must first discover if a performance problem exists. If it does exist, is the problem a lack of skills? If this is the case, which part of the skilled-performance process needs developing (Figure 2.3.)?

Motivation

Referring to the model in Figure 2.3, we can start with motivation. If motivation is a problem, this may be a result of factors either within the individual or in the person's environment. Internal factors might include:

- lack of knowledge and skills to do the job properly
- general low self-esteem
- dislike for job, lack of satisfaction from job
- lack of personal goals, lack of ambition.

External factors might include:

- lack of proper training
- poor working conditions
- poor management and poor communication of corporate objectives, or corporate objectives at variance with individuals' objectives
- insufficient reward package
- monotonous job
- lack of opportunity to advance.

A problem of motivation may manifest itself through:

- absenteeism
- tardiness
- turnover of staff
- accidents and stoppages.

Specific ways of assessing attitude and motivation will be discussed later in this book (Chapter 5). Suffice to say here that individuals' attitudes are of fundamental importance to skilled performances within the workplace, and therefore for meeting operational objectives.

Nothing gets done in an organization without a conscious decision being made by a human being. If motivational problems are not addressed properly then other factors within the skilled performances in an organization will be largely ineffective. These problems can be addressed in a number of ways, not all by training. Examples are:

- goal setting
- participating in decision making
- incentive schemes.

(See McCormick and Ilgen, 1985, for more details of these particular approaches.)

Perception

Returning to the skills model in Figure 2.3, perception is the first type of skill to be brought into effect in a skilled performance. We must know what we are looking for (knowledge) and we must have the ability and skills to comprehend information in the context of the work being undertaken. A prerequisite therefore is knowledge of the job. Specific knowledge can be identified for each job, and incorporated in training for that job.

The skills required can also be identified. To help in this, Berliner (1964) gives a 'classificatory scheme' for human performance, and identifies specific behaviours associated with the perceptual process under two headings as follows.

Searching for and receiving information:
detects
inspects
observes
reads
receives
scans
surveys.

Identifying objects, actions and events:
discriminates
identifies
locates.

These categories can be used to help identify specific perceptual skills required in any job. There are a number of ways to develop perceptual skills but these are not specifically dealt with here (see Jackson, 1989).

Translation

Referring to Figure 2.3, the 'translation' process is a cognitive (or 'thinking') one which requires a combination of knowledge and skills: knowing what to do with the information perceived, and the ability to translate this into action. The latter involves first information-processing skills, and secondly decision-making and problem-solving skills. Berliner (1964) calls these 'mediational processes', and categorizes associated behaviours as follows:

Information processing:
   categorizes
   calculates
   codes
   computes
   interpolates
   itemizes
   tabulates
   translates

Problem solving and decision making:
   analyses
   calculates
   chooses
   compares
   computes
   estimates
   plans.

Again, it is possible to identify translation skills required in each job by reference to this classification, and to identify the knowledge required to enable job holders to process information and make decisions.

Behaviour

Referring to Figure 2.3, we can again turn to Berliner (1964) to help identify the specific skills necessary to make an impression on our environment – that is, those actions we take which are observable and are capable of producing change.

Berliner (1964) divides observable behaviour into 'communication processes' and 'motor processes'. Communication processes are those actions we take to influence our social environment (for example manage staff) and motor processes are those actions we take to influence or change our physical environment (for example process work or manufacture an item). The specific behaviour categories are as follows.

Communication process:
  advises
  answers
  communicates
  directs
  indicates
  informs
  instructs
  requests
  transmits.

Motor process:
  adjusts
  aligns
  regulates
  synchronizes
  tracks
  activates
  closes
  connects
  disconnects
  joins
  moves
  presses
  sets.

It is these observable behaviours which are easier to detect and assess. However, it is easy to forget about motivation, perception and translation skills which are difficult to assess because they are not immediately observable. If these are forgotten, then it is difficult to detect the problem areas when a skilled-performance deficit exists.

Changes in the outside world

The final aspect of the skills model in Figure 2.3 is 'changes in the outside world'. These are the effects we have on the environment, either social or physical. They are *outcomes* of our behaviour, and are stated as accomplishments, as in the examples which follow.

Operational outcomes:
Eg
   units produced
   items assembled
   items sold
   copies completed
   purchases made
   forms processed.

Problems of performance are to be discovered in these outcomes rather than in the *process* of skilled performances. However, the causes of and solutions to problems are to be found in the process itself. By analysing the skilled performance as we have done, by looking at motivation, perception, translation and behaviour, we can isolate skills problems and address them by training.

Finally, how do we know when skilled performances are in line with operational (and therefore corporate) objectives, and how do we know when there is a performance problem? We look at the difference between what is required to achieve targets, and what the actual situation is (Figure 1.2). Before we can begin the *evaluation phase* we need to establish 'base-line data' (see Figure 1.1) (this is discussed further in Chapter 3). However, before we go any further it may be wise to summarize the *diagnostic phase*.

Summary of the diagnostic process

To be successful in evaluating training and development programmes, we must make sure that they are directed at corporate objectives. This. is only possible by completing a diagnostic phase which identifies:

- corporate objectives
- what is being done, or must be done, operationally to achieve corporate objectives
- what skills are required to achieve operationally those objectives which are in line with corporate objectives.

By looking at the difference between what is and what ought to be at operational level, we can determine whether there is a need to close the 'performance gap'. This may focus on current performance or future performance depending on the objectives (corporate and operational) being addressed. By looking at the 'skilled performance' processes at operational level we can assess where in each process we need to address skills and knowledge, or whether we need to address a motivational problem.

This is the basis upon which we can now write training objectives directed at developing the skilled performance, and upon which we can establish base-line data (actual performance) against targets (required performance). Targets are standards for skilled performances which give us criteria against which performance can be judged. Let us look at how this works against corporate objectives in an example (Figure 2.4).

	Example
Corporate goal	Increase market share
Corporate objective	Improve quality of customer service by reducing complaints and reducing closures of accounts
Operational objective of line manager	Reduce number of complaints from customers by 10%
What staff need to do to meet this target – standards	Process application within 24 hours No errors No referrals to supervisor unless the following conditions exist: applicant non-resident application above £50,000

Figure 2.4 Standards drawn from corporate objectives

If our base-line performance data are below these standards then there is a performance gap. If it is possible to close this gap by developing skills, there is a training need.

Throughout this chapter, certain assumptions have been made. Specifically, we have assumed that you will be able successfully to complete the diagnostic phase, although the various problems in doing this have been discussed. It may be the case that you are unable to do this, or that you are a current provider of training and want to check whether your programmes give financial benefit to the organization or organizations you serve. You may like to start from the bottom (skills level) and work up towards the corporate objectives level. Chapter 3 provides a way of doing this by looking at the diagnostic process in reverse: we call this the *evaluation phase*.

3. The evaluation process

A template for evaluation

At this stage in the 'evaluation cycle', comprising diagnosis and now evaluation, we will make the assumption that you have successfully identified corporate objectives, operational objectives and skills requirements; that you have written objectives for your training courses and run them; and that you now wish to assess the impact you have had on your organization or client organization. Alternatively, we can assume that you have not completed the diagnostic phase and wish to jump straight into evaluation. It is possible to jump into the cycle at this stage as a short cut although there are dangers in this. At some time you will still need to identify operational and corporate objectives if you are to complete the cycle.

The template in Figure 3.1 is really an inversion of the diagnostic template. It approaches the process from the bottom up, rather than the top down.

By the end of this chapter you should know how to use the template in Figure 3.1. This should help you to develop an evaluation strategy.

Applying skills in the workplace

You have run a course and participants have learned and practised certain skilled performances in the classroom. What next? What do they do with these skills? Why have they learnt them? How are they going to use them in the workplace to affect operational results? Let us start at the beginning, work through the template, and see if we can come up with some answers to these questions.

From the diagnostic phase you have derived objectives for your training programme. Objectives should indicate as a minimum:

- the skills you are to develop in students

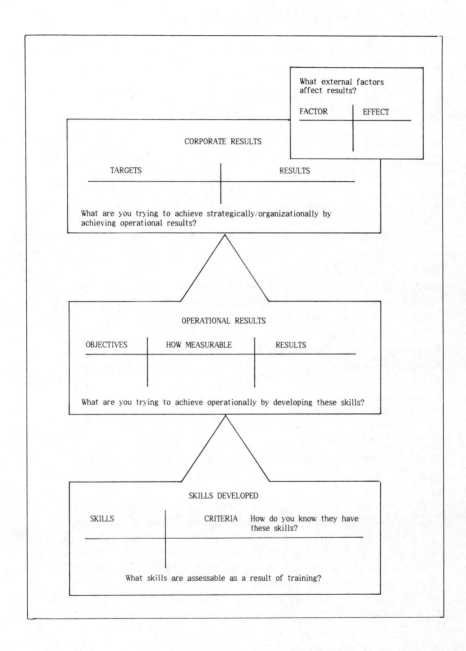

Figure 3.1 Template for evaluation

- how you know when they have acquired and successfully applied those skills in the workplace.

These training objectives should be linked to operational objectives by your stating:

- the expected operational impact of applying those skills
- the corporate objectives towards which they are aimed.

It is only possible to derive these objectives if you have been through the diagnostic phase, as your ultimate objective is to show a contribution to achieving corporate objectives. This is therefore your starting point. From this you can derive the operational objectives you need to be addressing, and from this the skilled performances needed to meet operational objectives.

What if you are running a course which addresses generic skills such as a management skills course? Let us use this as an example of how we can start at the skills level and work upwards to the operational level. The secret is to use the words what, how and why.

First, *what* skills are you attempting to develop in course participants? Your answer might include the following:

- work planning and managing own time
- creative thinking
- problem identification and solving
- decision making
- spoken communication.

Second, *how* do you know when these skills have been successfully applied in the workplace? Working with the course participants and their line management, you may come up with answers similar to those in Figure 3.2.

The criteria listed in Figure 3.2 will determine whether students have gone back to the workplace and have applied their new skills.

Thirdly, *why* do you want to develop these skills in course participants? This brings us back to the diagnostic phase. You want to develop skills to produce a better-skilled performance and to meet both operational and corporate objectives. You will not know whether you are on course, or indeed, the point of developing the skills, unless you have undertaken some diagnostic work to identify:

- corporate and operational objectives
- how performance should be improved
- what skills need to be developed to improve performance.

Skills	*How do you know when employees have applied these skills?*
Work planning/ time management	Has increased effective use of own time, showing time savings on work done
Creativity	Has created new ways of doing work to increase time savings, volume and/or quality of work
Problem solving	Has improved problem identification and solving, avoiding errors and wasted time
Decision making	Has improved timeliness and quality of decisions made, saving time and costs, reducing errors/ improving quality
Spoken communication	Has conveyed ideas and information more clearly, improving quality of work and saving time
Written communication	Has conveyed ideas and information more clearly and quickly, saving time in drafting and improving quality of work
Developing rapport	Has established relationships with others more quickly, improving working relationships and achieving improved quality in results
Negotiating	Has increased acceptability to the parties concerned of outcome of negotiations and in so doing has achieved own objectives
Motivating others	Has increased staff motivation and enthusiasm for work, producing quicker, higher-quality results
Managing stress	Has coped better with high volumes of work and strict deadlines, while maintaining good relations with others, who in turn opt out less
Team working	Has cooperated better with others, obtaining quicker, better-quality results
Developing team members	Has increased skills and knowledge of team members, producing quicker, better-quality results
Planning work of others	Has organized work of team better, increasing work flow and quality and timeliness of output
Delegating	Has distributed work downwards better, ensuring quicker and better-quality team results
Leading	Has led team more effectively, ensuring sustained, quicker and better-quality results

Figure 3.2 Criteria for generic management skills

If you have not undertaken this basic diagnostic work, this may lead to what Goldstein (1986, page 117) calls 'criteria deficiency'. This is where criteria identified in a diagnostic process are not present in the criteria used for identifying changes in performance following a training programme. Similarly, if needs have not been properly identified prior to the training programme, there is likely to be a deficiency in the criteria used. So, while we can derive criteria from working backwards from skills development offered in existing courses, we do not know if they are the criteria required to meet operational objectives. This is particularly the case when we are not dealing with a set of generic skills (such as management skills) but with *task*-specific skills. A *task* is a skilled performance of a particular complexity (see page 29) depending on the nature of the task and the skills and knowledge required to perform the task, and is related to a specific job. *Skilled performance* has a wider meaning. It includes tasks, but also encompasses social performance which is not necessarily related to a particular job.

Skilled performances within particular jobs can be grouped within *key results areas*. These are the key functions of a job which are instrumental in producing results for the organization in line with corporate objectives. There are, of course, areas of any job which are not particularly productive and not in line with corporate objectives, and by identifying which areas these are, jobs can be better targeted towards achieving corporate objectives.

Criteria for successful skilled performances are of two different types: *process* criteria and *outcome* criteria (Goldstein, 1986). Referring again to Figure 2.3, we can see that to produce outcomes (changes in the outside world) process skills of perception, translation and behaviour are required. It is possible to identify the skills which are needed for the successful completion of the skilled performance. Process criteria are measures of whether or not skills exist and to what extent, and when those criteria are not met this is the main indicator of training needs.

In developing process criteria we can construct a *profile of skills requirements* by identifying each key results area, and then identifying the skills and knowledge required to achieve results in these areas. It is then necessary to assess the extent to which the individual has these skills (see Chapter 4). Figure 3.3, for example, provides a classification of skills for clerical and managerial skilled performances. Appropriate skills can be selected from this for each key results area identified.

Actions change the environment in some way, and it is possible to assess these *outcomes*. The way we do this provides *outcome criteria*, and these lead us into the *operational level* of evaluation as actions produce operational results. However, as we have seen in Figure 3.2, it is only really possible to provide criteria for application of skills in the workplace by reference to the outcomes of actions that have been taken in the workplace using the skills learned. To make sure that it is the

Perception: Obtaining and Understanding Information

1. Concentrating on task in a distracting environment
2. Obtaining information by listening to people
3. Obtaining information from a computer
4. Obtaining information by observing work processes
5. Understanding technical information from written material relevant to job
6. Scanning and understanding a table of figures
7. Understanding statistical information
8. Selecting relevant information from irrelevant information
9. Identifying appropriate sources of information
10. Identifying errors in own work
11. Identifying errors and problems in others' work
12. Listening to people understandingly and sympathetically

Translation: Processing Information and Ideas

13. Copying information from one form to another
14. Sorting information into different categories
15. Tabulating information
16. Memorizing information
17. Planning own work
18. Obtaining information in order to make decisions
19. Identifying problems needing action
20. Choosing between different ideas and actions
21. Judging own work
22. Judging quality of information available
23. Solving mathematical problems
24. Estimating or projecting from available information and/or figures
25. Analysing information or data
26. Using general principles to solve specific problems
27. Judging others' work
28. Planning others' work
29. Setting own goals
30. Generating new ideas and different approaches to problem solving
31. Considering influence of organizational structure, functions and culture in decision making
32. Setting others' goals

Behaviour: Actions

33. Carrying objects
34. Using a keyboard
35. Controlling/using equipment
36. Following procedures
37. Sorting information or objects into categories
38. Explaining, orally, aspects of work
39. Explaining, in writing, aspects of work

40.   Managing own time
41.   Answering questions
42.   Giving feedback to superiors/subordinates
43.   Advising others
44.   Giving instructions
45.   Negotiating with others
46.   Directing others' work
47.   Teaching others
48.   Talking to groups of people
49.   Implementing a plan
50.   Supervising others
51.   Delegating work
52.   Scheduling work
53.   Coordinating others' activities
54.   Conducting meetings
55.   Selecting employees
56.   Handling grievances/problems
57.   Maintaining a working atmosphere

Figure 3.3 Classification of clerical and managerial skills

training that is impacting on outcomes, though, we must first establish that our training programme produced a development in skills which were subsequently applied in the workplace to produce enhanced results. Process criteria must therefore be developed by identifying:

- what skills are required to do the job
- how you can tell whether or not individuals have those skills.

The extent to which individuals have those skills before and after training can then be determined by *assessment* (of process) and/or *measurement* (of outcomes). Exactly how this may be tackled will be discussed in Chapter 4.

Let us now turn to the operational results we are trying to achieve by developing skills in individuals.

Achieving operational results

Results at operational level are obtained by inputting resources into an operational environment which produces output via a particular throughput system. Or simply:

Resources   Results

INPUT   - - - - - - - → THROUGHPUT - - - - - - - → OUTPUT

Resources put into the system are listed on page 27, and include physical and human resources, money, time and information. Training, which enhances the skills of people working within this environment, impacts on two main areas of inputs – *time* and *costs*– and it is these which we will be concentrating on later.

Training has largely to accept the physical resources available and cannot impact on them, unlike the resource of information where quality and availability can be affected by training. By affecting human resources, training can impact on the time needed to perform a task, and the actual cost of an operation.

The operational environment referred to above has been described in Chapter 2 as including structure, systems, resources and activities. Training alone does not directly affect structure and systems but may indirectly affect them if directed as strategic management level.

Outputs are what an operational process produces from the resources inputted. Outputs can be measured in terms of *volume* and *quality*. The word 'quantity' has been avoided here because often this is contrasted to quality, the latter being 'unquantifiable'. This is misleading as it is often possible to quantify quality through such measures as number of errors, scrap rate and rework.

Phillips describes the operational results discussed above as 'output increases' (volume), 'time savings', 'quality improvements' and 'cost savings' – these being the four major categories of 'hard data' which are 'the primary measurement of improvement, presented as rational undisputed facts' (Phillips, 1983, page 126). We can improve on this and classify these four areas into outputs and inputs as in Figure 3.4. Note that inputs can also be outputs, and outputs can be inputs! By following the direction of the arrows in Figure 3.4, the tails of the arrows can be inputs, and the points can be outputs (see also page 51).

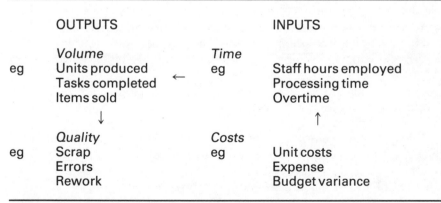

	OUTPUTS			INPUTS
	Volume		*Time*	
eg	Units produced	←	eg	Staff hours employed
	Tasks completed			Processing time
	Items sold			Overtime
	↓			↑
	Quality		*Costs*	
eg	Scrap		eg	Unit costs
	Errors			Expense
	Rework			Budget variance

Figure 3.4 Classification of outputs and inputs

Definitions of 'efficiency', 'effectiveness' and 'productivity' given on page 2 are relevant here, as it is at these that operational objectives are usually directed. Improvements in operational performance are directed towards reducing the inputs (efficiency), increasing the outputs (effectiveness), or both (productivity). We can therefore look at performance in terms of outputs per inputs; for example, the number of units produced per staff hours employed. Skilled performances, producing changes in the outside world (see Figure 2.3), involve demonstrable inputs and outputs.

Performances which do not produce demonstrable outputs (results) are neither skilled nor required in an organizational or business setting. The only complication in this is that for some skilled performances, particularly interpersonal performances, outputs may not be demonstrable immediately, and may only contribute to outputs alongside other factors. However, there are always immediate effects on the outside world as a result of actions we take, but some of these may only present themselves in what Phillips (1983) calls 'soft data'. For example, actions that managers take may result in immediate responses such as attitude changes, favourable reactions, enhanced loyalty and increased job satisfaction. These are difficult to measure immediately, but have a 'knock-on' effect with regard to factors such as absenteeism, lateness, staff turnover and grievances, which can be measured some time after the training event. We will look at the way attitude changes can be dealt with in Chapter 5.

We are therefore looking at 'output/outcome criteria' (see page 42) to determine the way in which enhanced skilled performances, following training, produce operational results; and we are trying to establish relationships between *skills* acquired as a result of training, enhanced *skills performance* in the workplace, and *operational results*. We have already discussed this at the skills level asking the questions:

- What skills are you attempting to develop in course participants?
- How do you know when they have successfully applied them?
- Why do you want to develop these skills in these individuals?

Let us now look at the questions we need to be asking about the specific job the course participant is employed to do and the way skills are used to produce operational results.

A major point to note is that jobs within an organization exist for a particular purpose: they are needed to perform the functions of the organization and to meet corporate objectives. The questions to ask of the job holder, with confirmation from the supervisor, are:

- Why does the organization need you in that position? To get what done: the *main function* of your job? (step 1)

- In order to perform this function what do you have to do? What are the main activities which produce results for the organization: your *key results areas?* (step 2)
- In each of these activities, how does your boss know whether to be happy with your work? What is the proof that you are doing what you say, and doing it well? (Step 3)
- How can your boss tell whether you have done a better job or a worse job from one month to the next? What are the measures of how well you are doing your job? (step 4)

Let us pause here for a moment and consider this last question. Supposing the job holder has replied, 'I have done my job well when:

- I have accurately entered data with no mistakes
- I have completed the work within the deadline
- I receive positive comments from customers on the service I provide.'

Or, 'Possible measures of how well I do in my job are:

- Number of accurate entries *per* amount of work processed
- Average completion time before deadline *per* amount of work processed
- Number of positive comments from customers *per* number of telephone calls taken.'

Note that both sides of the equation have been considered, as follows:

$$\frac{\text{effectiveness}}{\text{efficiency}} = \frac{\text{outputs}}{\text{inputs}} = \text{eg} \quad \frac{\text{No of accurate entries}}{\text{No of items processed}}$$

To continue with the questioning:

- Against the measures of how well you do your job, how well are you actually doing? What is your current achievement level? (If necessary keep records for a month.) (step 5)
- Are you (and your boss) satisfied with your current achievement level? Could it be improved? If so how? What steps do you need to take to increase your achievement in each of the key results areas? (step 6)
- If you take these steps (which may include skills development) how much do you think you could improve on last month's achievement level? What would be your objectives? (step 7).

So, we have really been through a diagnostic process to obtain performance measures. We did say above that the evaluation phase is an inversion of the diagnostic phase! Let us look at what we have now got. Figure 3.5 provides a proforma for recording measures of achievement.

NAME			POSITION		
FUNCTION Step 1					
KEY RESULTS AREAS Step 2	EVIDENCE OF GOOD JOB Step 3	MEASURES OF ACHIEVEMENT Step 4	CURRENT ACHIEVEMENT Step 5	STEPS NEEDED TO IMPROVE ACHIEVEMENT Step 6	GOALS Step 7
1.					
2.					
3.					
4.					
5.					
6.					

Figure 3.5 Measures of achievement in job

By completing the proforma 'Measures of achievement in job' in Figure 3.5, you should be able to answer the question posed in Figure 3.1: 'What are you trying to achieve operationally by developing these skills?' Your students should then be able to go back to their workplaces, armed with an action plan, and use the skills developed on your course to achieve operational results.

We said previously that this book is not the place within which to discuss course design, but let us just pause for thought a moment. Say you have line managers coming on your course. The purpose of the course might be to improve interpersonal skills. Why are they developing these skills? How are they going to use them when they go back to the line? To improve what? The first thing for these managers to think about is the job they do, its overall function and the main activities which are important for operational and corporate results. They then need to think about how they can tell (or their boss can tell) when they are doing a good job so they have some sort of 'benchmark' against which they can make a judgement about how well they are doing. It may be that they are doing a great job and should not really be wasting their time by being on your course!

Once the course participants know that they could be achieving more in their job, they can then start to look for the weaknesses, and what needs to be improved. Specifically, what interpersonal skills do they need to develop to improve the performance of their team? What do they need to do with these skills once back at work? Where do they need to direct their efforts? From this they have an action plan. They can develop within your course the interpersonal skills they really need in order to develop their team in the direction they need to go. They can then go back to the workplace with a definite plan of action, with specific objectives and definable targets. Armed with their benchmark (output criteria and ouput measures), which you have helped them to define, they can then see what improvement they have made in terms of operational results and how your course has helped them to do this. They will also get more satisfaction out of doing this, rather than simply being filled with the 'course euphoria' following a residential or external course which does not tend to last past the first day back at work.

By integrating this process into the course design you can ensure that skills learned in the classroom are directed towards operational results. The difficult part about completing this process is defining output criteria (measures of doing a job well). Figure 3.6 provides possible outputs for general job functions from which can be selected appropriate outputs. This provides one quarter of the equation: outputs by volume. The other quarters being outputs by quality; inputs of time; and inputs of costs.

---

1. Units produced
2. Items assembled
3. Items/money collected
4. Items sold
5. Forms/applications processed
6. Information sent
7. Items sent
8. Equipment maintained/mended
9. Documents typed
10. Documents filed

11. Correspondence sent
12. Diary kept
13. Orders taken
14. Invoices written
15. Cash deposited
16. Copies completed
17. Messages conveyed
18. Purchases made
19. Arrangements made
20. Salaries calculated

21. Enquiries made
22. Advertisements placed
23. Documents written
24. Statistics produced
25. Information produced
26. Records completed
27. Data processed
28. Stock recorded
29. Applications approved
30. Operations completed

31. Agreements gained
32. Administration completed
33. Systems designed
34. Systems produced
35. Problems solved
36. Projects completed
37. Decisions made/commitment gained
38. Ideas accepted/implemented
39. Advice given/accepted
40. Presentations made
41. Deals completed
42. Programmes designed/completed
43. Plans completed/accepted
44. Conflicts avoided/solved
45. Work scheduled
46. Proposals submitted/accepted
47. Meeting held
48. Appraisals completed
49. Budgets completed/agreed
50. Employees selected

51. Forecasts made
52. Clients gained
53. Staff trained

Figure 3.6 Possible outputs from general job functions

Quality can be measured. More accurately stated, deviations from the standard can be measured: indications of a lack of quality, or as Crosby (1979) has put it 'The cost of quality is the expense of doing things wrong'. More specifically, the cost of:

Failures
- doing work again
- scrap
- handling returns
- after-sales service and warrantees
- dealing with complaints
- redesign
- product liability
- errors generally
- loss of customer credibility and loss of customers.

There is also the cost of monitoring and supervising work in progress to prevent such failures. In particular this may be a problem where junior staff are inexperienced and not fully trained, resulting in supervisors having to inspect work frequently. In summary these are the costs in time of:

Appraisal
- inspection of work
- monitoring and supervision
- product tests
- process control
- reporting or errors.

The cost of prevention of errors and failures is the time and money spent on training, quality service programmes, design reviews, procedural and systems reviews, and quality audits, to name some of the approaches to quality improvement.

Although quality is often a 'qualitative' matter, that is, regarded as not being the subject of quantitative measurement, particularly in professional occupations, a lack of quality or non-conformity to accepted standards of work (from a customer viewpoint) will always result in more work for somebody, usually the supervisor, loss of credibility and loss of customers. This is measurable.

The quality of work (output) can be compared with the volume of work (in this case regarded as the input; see also page 47) and combined in a ratio statement such as number of errors per 1,000 units produced, number of complaints per 100 customers or amount of rework per 100 documents processed. This gives a total measure of outputs in volume and quality.

Inputs into the system which must be considered alongside outputs are time and costs, as we have seen above. A measure of time is simply the number of staff hours taken to produce certain outcomes. This also includes supervisory time. It can also be the reverse of this: the amount of unproductive time such as downtime, travelling time, unscheduled breaks, absenteeism and lateness. Included within unproductive time is the 'learning curve' when the trainee is learning the job. At the beginning the new trainee is largely unproductive, goes through stages of partially productive time, until fully productive when the training has been successfully completed. A method for costing the learning curve will be discussed in Chapter 5. Time, of course, is a cost. Other costs include the fixed costs of offices, factories, plant and equipment, on which training has little impact; variable costs of services (including training) and materials, on which training can have an impact. Opportunity costs are not usually shown in accounting systems, but represent the income forgone as a result of rejecting an alternative. This can be the cost of wrong decision making or the cost of not having the wherewithal to take advantage of an opportunity. This is important in calculating the cost of not training and is taken up in Chapter 5.

We have looked at the implications to operational results of developing skills in the classroom. It is likely that the higher up the line the course participant is, the more the impact on the organization that individual is likely to have when applying skills learned to skilled performances in the workplace. The criteria of management performance are the results produced by the work group under that person, rather than individual managerial results producing 'soft data' in Phillips' (1983) phraseology. In some ways, therefore, it is easier to show the impact of management skills training than staff or technical training as the overall impact on the organization can be greater.

Let us assume that your training course has developed skills which participants have taken back to the workplace, applied, and which have produced operational results. Good, but what are the implications for achieving corporate objectives? Let us now turn to our third level of evaluation: corporate results.

Meeting corporate objectives

What are you trying to achieve organizationally by arriving at operational results? Which corporate objectives are being addressed? To what extent has training and development contributed to achieving corporate results?

Your responsibility within the organization probably begins and ends with training and development, although you may have other human resource responsibilities. Remember, we have said that training and development are tools which the line can draw upon as appropriate.

They are not bound by these tools, they can use others, and they do not have to follow through on your training initiatives. You have no specific operational responsibility, and the results achieved operationally are the responsibility of the line. You do not, therefore, have the responsibility for ensuring that the training you do yields results operationally and organizationally (although the finger will probably point at you if your training is of no value to the line).

It is when the course participant, now back in the workplace, starts to apply skills that you begin to lose control. Other factors creep in which may either undo your good work, or may positively impact on performance over and above the effect of training. If you have gone through the diagnosis process, you should be well aware of those other factors impacting on the achievement of operational results and corporate objectives. Let us just recap on what those other factors might be by asking you to be aware of what is happening in your organization.

At operational level

Has the structure of the organization been changed? This may be to reflect better the marketing stance of the company, as a result of a redefinition of the markets the company is in, or to help work and information flow throughout the organization to respond better to the needs of clients and customers.

Have new systems been introduced? A new computer system may have a dramatic effect on performance, but rely heavily on the training input for success.

Have resources (physical or human) been increased, decreased or otherwise changed so as to impact on the general performance of the organization or part of it? Simply taking on more staff would have an effect on overall performance of an operational unit, providing these staff were sufficiently trained. Additional office or factory accommodation may enable the taking on of more business or an increase in production.

Have the activities of the organization changed in any way? Marketing, financial control, production, and research and development activities might all significantly impact on performance. However, any change in activities of this nature will require the input of training to develop new skills.

At corporate level

Has the organization itself changed in any way by means of merger, acquisition or change of ownership or control? This may have implications for the way the organization does business or the way it is managed.

Has there been a change in the environment in which the organization operates? Shifts in the market or the economy, such as a stock market crash, or the availability of consumer credit, may affect the market position of the company and the way it performs. Similarly, government policy or legislation may significantly impact on the performance of organizations in specific industrial sectors. In December 1988 the informal comments of a junior health minister in the British Government had a dramatic adverse effect on egg producers.

Has there been a change in the input of resources into the organization? This may be dependent on the two above factors: ownership and environment. A change of ownership or a stock exchange listing may provide more capital input. Environmental factors, such as the predicted shortage of UK school leavers in the 1990s, may affect the input of human resources into organizations. (See, for example, Kubr, 1980, pages 65–72, for factors considered in management audits which impact on performance.)

The extent to which these factors impact on operational and corporate results can be determined in much the same way as the extent of training's impact on results can be determined: by building up, step by step, a chain of connections.

It is particularly difficult to build up a *causal* chain from skills to operational results to corporate results. Social, economic and behavioural scientists have tended to rely on *correlations* between activities and events as the best possible connecting link between events, particularly those involving human beings where a whole myriad of factors may impact on results. A causal link is a relationship between one event and another, the latter resulting from the former. A correlation simply implies that when you have one event the other event is also present. With so many factors present which might 'cause' the organization to achieve certain results, it is difficult to identify positively which factor caused which result.

However, what we are saying in this book is that if you target certain management efforts towards specific corporate objectives and results are achieved at each stage from skills, behaviour at work, operational results and meeting corporate objectives (establishing a correlation between these events); and if you can allow for other factors by identifying them and estimating their impact on corporate results, then you can establish that the specific management efforts have contributed to corporate results in such a way that their financial impact can be appraised. In Figure 1.3 we tackled this problem at an early stage by giving examples of evaluation design which serve to isolate the effects of other factors impacting on an improvement in performance.

There are statistical methods which can be used to calculate the relative 'strengths' of correlations between each of a number of *independent* variables (those factors impacting on the result), *intervening* variables (those factors which mediate between independent variables and the end result) and *dependent* variables (the result which is dependent on the factors above). Such a method is *path analysis*, described by de Vaus (1986), where the correlation coefficients between factors are used to 'weight' the relationship between factors in a 'causal' path from independent variables to intervening variables to dependent variables (the result).

Let us simplify this by using terminology employed by Likert (1987) which corresponds to the three types of variables described above, and apply this in Figure 3.7 to the three levels of our analysis: skills, operational results and corporate results. Again, the calculations of the relationships between variables have been kept simple by asking managers for estimates of the contribution of each factor identified to the end result. This is quite often possible and, if agreement can be gained, management commitment to the figures they themselves provide is ensured. In the example in Figure 3.7, 90 per cent of the causal variables contribute to operational results in the proportions indicated, and one causal factor (contributing 10 per cent to the end

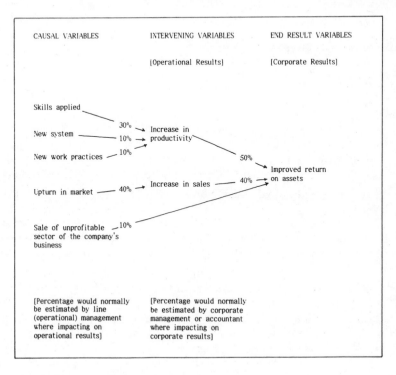

Figure 3.7 Simple path analysis

result) impacts directly on the end-result variable.

We have mentioned above the use of ratio analysis in providing an indication of organizational performance. This is a useful way of showing a connection between operational results and corporate results. For example, as trainers we are particularly interested in the contribution of human resources to end results. By providing skills training to production staff and to sales staff the following results should accrue.

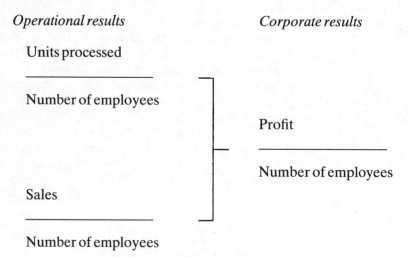

Operational results   *Corporate results*

Units processed
_____

Number of employees
                                                        Profit
                                                        _____
                                                        Number of employees
Sales
_____

Number of employees

Although such ratios do not prove a causal connection between operational and corporate results, they do provide evidence of a positive and strong correlation between the two. Any evaluation strategy should therefore seek to show the connection between variables, from the factors over which the trainer has some control (skills development), to factors where there are other variables impacting over which the trainer has no control. It is necessary to isolate these other factors so the relative contributions of each variable can be demonstrated.

The last two chapters have provided a template for evaluation strategy. In many ways this has been a 'broad brush' treatment of a process which requires of the trainer a wide range of knowledge and skills. The following chapters provide more detail on some of the issues which specifically concern trainers.

Chapter 4 deals with the issue of how to assess individual performance, and chapter 5 looks at methods for showing the financial implications of training and development.

Part 3
Evaluation methods

4. Measuring the performance gap

Measurement and assessment

In the last two chapters we have concentrated on an overview of evaluation, and on fitting evaluation in with operational and corporate objectives. Here we look at the behavioural end – assessment – to develop methods of measuring the 'performance gap' of individuals and work groups. This is a major obstacle. If you cannot measure accurately how well people are performing in their jobs before training, you are not going to be able to determine what impact the training has had on their performance.

Let us first define our terms as we have used both 'assessment' and 'measurement' casually up until now. The following analogy with sport is useful in explaining these terms (this idea from Coonradt, 1985). The performance of a soccer team is easy to *measure*. It is the number of goals scored. Results are *measurable* by counting the number of times the ball is put in the net. This is a fairly objective method, apart from a 'quality control' aspect which depends on the judgement of the referee and linesmen who ensure that the process of getting the goals is a fair one with no breaching of the rules.

Not so straightforward is the *assessment* of performance in gymnastics. There are no actual results: no units by which to measure performance. Expert opinion takes the place of counting measurable units. This is not so 'objective' as scoring goals in football, but it works because:

- everyone agrees on the basic criteria for assessment
- the opinion of the expert panel of judges is respected.

If we look at these two methods of determining performance more closely, we can distinguish:

- assessment of *process* (gymnastics analogy)
- measurement of *outcome* (soccer analogy).

In gymnastics there is no outcome as such, other than the performance itself. It is the performance which is judged rather than any product or outcome. In soccer, there is a definite outcome: the number of goals scored by each team: the team with the higher score wins.

Performance in some jobs is easily measurable by counting actual results (for example, units produced or value of sales). In other jobs, principally clerical and professional work, it is not always possible to count units of production and it may be easier to concentrate on the assessment of the process of the skilled performance. Assessment, based on expert opinion and shared criteria, may be used successfully to determine the 'gap' between actual performance and required performance. This may be carried out under the following conditions:

- Assessment is undertaken by the recognized 'expert(s)'. This would normally be the immediate supervisor who is familiar with the work of the staff assessed and knows what is expected of the assessee in terms of work performance, and is recognized by both staff and management to have this knowledge.
- All (staff, supervisor, managers) agree on the criteria for assessment: they agree on what is required to do the job well. Agreement and commitment to the criteria can be gained by combining the supervisor's assessment with the staff's assessment of themselves, by discussing the criteria and obtaining agreement.
- Staff (the assessees) are involved in the assessment process. This differs from the analogy with gymnastics, but is extremely important for training. Self assessment engenders a commitment to self development.

Self assessment is an aspect which is often forgotten as it is seen as too 'subjective'. However, if individuals can examine their strengths and weaknesses and determine their own training needs with the help of their supervisors, and if they can set objectives to meet performance requirements, this can provide a tremendous motivational impetus. Individuals' own objectives are far more motivating than those laid down and enforced by other people. Individuals are far more likely to want to close the performance gap if they have identified it themselves (although to be in line with corporate objectives there must be good communication within the organization).

Self assessment is often seen as being biased in favour of the assessee whereas supervisor assessment is sometimes seen as possibly biased against an unfavoured employee or towards a favoured one. However, there is increasing research evidence to suggest that where there is good communication and performance feedback between supervisor and staff, self and supervisor assessment of staff largely agree. Where staff are asked to assess themselves as they would expect their supervisor to assess them, then agreement between self and supervisor is good. Where staff are assessing themselves for training purposes, there is good agreement with other methods of performance assessment. Where self assessment is going to be used for staff reporting purposes, and particularly where it is linked with pay, self assessment is not necessarily accurate. (See for example McEnery and McEnery, 1987. Other recent reports of research findings on self and supervisor assessment include Ford and Noe, 1987; and, Yammarino, Dubinsky and Hartley, 1987.) Supervisor assessment may well be biased. However, there is much evidence to suggest that attitudes of supervisors have an influence on the performance of staff. Where the supervisor consistently expects staff to perform badly, they probably will (self-fulfilling prophecy is explained in more detail in Burns, 1979, pages 286–94). A combination of supervisor and staff assessment of performance should be used. Where possible, performance ratings thus obtained should be corroborated with other methods, and be correlated with outcomes of performance.

We have already spent some time in Chapter 4 looking at measures of outcomes in terms of ratio analysis. By definition, a measure is a quantity. Typical numeric measures of individual and group performance are volume of work per number of staff hours and number of errors per volume of work. There is a further way that performance can be assessed: by looking at the potential of somebody to perform. Again, this is concerned with assessment, concentrates on the process of performance, but tries to make a prediction on how a particular person might perform. A footballer is selected by a team manager on the basis of the performance he is expected to give. This is usually done on the basis of the perceived *ability* of the player judged on past performance.

In a business setting, an individual's ability may be assessed in a number of ways to determine his or her potential within a job. These include, among others, personality, aptitude and ability testing by psychometric and assessment-centre techniques for assessing the potential of job applicants; performance-appraisal methods such as judgement of current performance and 'traits' or perceived aptitude for progression within an organization (employment appraisal schemes). These, essentially, focus on what is required to perform in a particular job, and try to fit the right person to the job.

In summary, there are three ways of looking at performance:

- the *potential* to perform
- the performance *process* itself
- the *outcome* of the performance.

The *value* of a performance to an organization is its outcome. The value of any predictive method is its ability to predict accurately the end result of a process: *predictive validity*. For example, if a selection method can be used which predicts more accurately than other methods which candidates will perform well in the job, the value of the method is the difference between results achieved by the selected candidates and those that would have been achieved by candidates selected using the old method. This may sound a bit complicated, but the relative 'utility' (see for example Cascio, 1982) of a selection method can be determined by using control group methods (described in Figure 1.3).

Predicting potential performance is also important in developing staff and managers. The value of a development programme is largely in the results obtained by the programme's participants sometime in the future. *Current performance* can be both assessed and measured by looking at the process and outcome of the performance, and this is our starting point in measuring the performance gap.

Current performance

Chapter 2 discussed the diagnostic phase of evaluation which aims to establish whether there is a shortfall between current performance and required performance, to discover the nature of this shortfall, and to determine the extent to which it can be addressed by training.

To establish whether there is a training need, a first step should be to measure the shortfall in performance. There are practical problems in measuring this performance deficit, some of which were indicated in Chapter 2. First, corporate and operational objectives may not be clearly defined, and therefore the performance required of departments, sections of departments, work groups or individuals may not be very clear. Second, this may mean that there are inadequately defined performance standards. This is really an operational problem rather than a training one. However, a trainer can assist in helping the line define expectations of performance and in setting targets and performance criteria if the diagnostic process has been carried out. Third, once criteria for performance are adequately defined, there is a problem in measuring the gap in performance accurately. For manufacturing industry, units actually produced against targeted production of units can be accurately measured. In sales, actual sales against targeted sales can be measured.

But what about office-based work? How can the performance of individuals here be measured accurately? One approach is to relate performance standards to the norms of the group and the norms of the industry. This may not go down well with those who have worked hard over the last few years to establish criterion-referenced instruction in contrast to norm-referenced instruction within training (see for example Mager and Pipe, 1976). However, corporate objectives and operational standards are usually related to the norms of the industry and dictates of the marketplace: that is, what an organization has to do to be competitive in the marketplace; how successful a company is compared with competitors; how cost-effective a public sector organization is compared with other such organizations. Corporate objectives should be set accordingly.

How effective is the department, section or other operational unit compared with other such units performing a similar role (for example, branches of a bank or a retail organization, allowing for differences in geographic location, size and other factors which might affect market performance)? Operational objectives should be set accordingly.

Similarly, individuals within the workplace can be seen in this way, and indeed often are when it comes to promotion: the best person for the job is selected on the basis of their performance and potential compared with their peers. However, having said this, measures of performance are never totally norm-referenced. Particularly in simple, routine jobs, or highly standardized production-type work, a person can either perform certain tasks or not. In high-level work such as managerial or professional jobs, the situation is not so straightforward as there are varying degrees of performance which are not based on a simple 'can do' or 'can't do' of particular tasks.

The following approach is illustrative of a combination of norm- and criterion-referenced assessment, which focuses on the process of performance rather than directly on outcome. It uses assessment ratings of self and supervisor to gain a profile of a work group, and to put a 'valuation' on the work group.

Individuals within an operational unit can be ranked using the ranked pair method: best/worst, second best/second worst, third best/third worst, and so on. This will provide a cluster around the norm: that is, most individuals will fall somewhere in the middle to give an average performance rating and provide a level of competency (tied to particular performance criteria) which is normal within the operating unit, and will give an average for the operational units within the organization, and an average for the organization within the industry. To draw performance criteria from this data, what the top performers do and what they possess in skills and knowledge should be identified. What the worst performers lack should also be determined. Similarly, what do the average performers achieve and with what skills and knowledge do they achieve it? Is the average performance adequate to meet operational and corporate objectives?

Criteria can thus be developed for performance standards (outcomes) and skills and knowledge required in line with operational and corporate objectives, related to the norms of the industry. If the average performance of the operational unit falls short of the norms for the industry, and is likely to fall short of objectives where these are clearly defined, the standards for individuals should be shifted upwards of the individual performance norm to represent a suitable industrial standard.

Once performance standards are defined, the number of individuals within the operational unit who do not reach the required standard can be assessed on the level of performance related to the norm. Those performing above the standard can similarly be assessed on their level of performance relative to the norm. The spread of individuals in each band of performance indicates the deficit (or surfeit) in performance within the operational unit. This is illustrated in Figure 4.1 which shows the distribution of staff at each level of performance from 0 (low) to 2 (high).

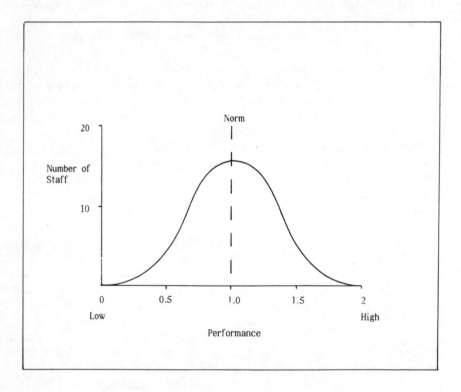

Figure 4.1 Performance distribution curve

A shortfall in performance means a shortfall in the value of an organization's human resources. Those staff performing consistently below the norm are clearly not giving the value which those performing above the norm are. We take here a premise which has been put forward by Cascio and Ramos (1986, page 20): that is 'the classic economic principle that the value of a commodity is its market price. The value of an individual's labour is equivalent to what an organization is willing to pay in order to obtain it'.

If job holders are performing to the standards and criteria laid down by the organization, if they are competent in the job, then their value to the organization is the price the organization pays for their time. If they are not performing competently, then they are not worth their cost to the organization. If they are only doing half of what they are supposed to do, or if they are taking twice as long to do the job as they should, they are only worth 50 per cent of their cost to the organization.

If assessment or measurement can be made accurately, related to the norm of the work group and performance criteria laid down by the organization (average performers and what is expected of them for the money they are paid), this can be related to a person's human resource value to the organization: the cost of not training.

After implementing a training programme, the performance gap can be measured again to see how far it has closed: to determine the increase in value of human resources. This concept is not being used here to establish a system of human resource accounting (see Flamholtz, 1974), but to show that trained personnel are valuable to an organization; and conversely, not training staff properly can cost money. If a large proportion of personnel are performing below the industrial norm, or not meeting criteria, this puts a company at a serious competitive disadvantage. If someone is performing at 50 per cent, somebody else has to be employed to make up the 50 per cent shortfall. This costs money!

Let us now look in more detail at the *grid analysis* method, used to 'anchor' individual and group performance both to the norm of the group and to performance criteria.

The performance grid

To perform effectively within an organization an individual requires:

- *skills* to enable the successful execution of a task
- *motivation* to be willing to perform the task
- *opportunity* within the organization to use the skills.

Skills level is usually judged on the quality of outcome and the efficiency, speed and ease with which that outcome is achieved. Motivation is judged on the basis of a person's energy level, enthusiasm, perseverence, concentration and conscientiousness. Opportunity is a function of the operational arrangements within an organization (structure, systems, resources and activities: see Chapter 2), driven by corporate and operational objectives, and involves the climate and culture of the organization and the styles of management. In many respects it also reflects the human resource practices within an organization: is the right person in the right job at the right time?

To assess the current performance of a work group it is necessary to obtain information on the two dimensions of skills and motivation, and on how these two combine in individuals' performances to lead to the results they achieve. However, we are not at this stage directly measuring outcomes. To assess potential performance it is necessary to match the third dimension, opportunity, with the abilities of an individual to develop and progress.

Here we are concerned with current performance – we will be looking at potential performance later (pages 75–8). This method requires the work group's supervisor to place all staff on a 'performance grid' along skills and motivation levels dimensions using the ranked pair method described on page 63. This grid is shown in Figure 4.2.

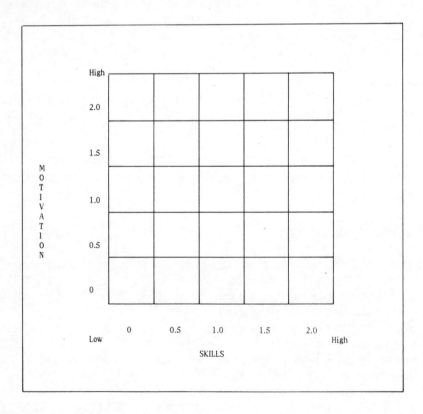

Figure 4.2 The performance grid

Probably the most famous 'grid' is the management grid of Blake and Mouton (1978). The use of grids is usefully explored in an article by Newstrom (1987). The idea of the grid shown in Figure 4.2 comes from Stewart (1986). Using this grid, the supervisor is asked to identify the best performer and worst performer and to place them both on the performance grid by reference to their motivation level and skills level, where 2 is the best they have ever known and 0 is the worst they have ever known. Staff new to the job may therefore have a low skills level, but a high level of motivation. They will therefore be placed towards the top left-hand corner of the grid. This process is repeated, second best/second worst, third best/third worst, and so on.

Additional guidance can be given to supervisors by providing *behavioural anchors* for each measure on the two scales. Examples are shown in Figure 4.3.

Current Performance

Skills dimension

0   No skills or knowledge currently to undertake present job

0.5   Some skills and knowledge, but not sufficient to do current job to the required standard

1   Sufficient skills and knowledge to do the job to the required standard

1.5   Sufficient skills and knowledge to do the job to a higher than required standard

2   Has a high level of skills and knowledge and can do the job to a very high standard

Motivation dimension

0   Has no interest in the work, no motivation, and therefore unable to perform adequately

0.5   Is sometimes motivated by the work, shows concentration, but requires more enthusiasm and energy successfully to complete the work

1   Sufficient motivation to get the job done

1.5   Often is highly motivated, with energy and enthusiasm. Can motivate others if required

2   A very high degree of motivation, showing great enthusiasm, energy and perseverance. Motivates others

---

Figure 4.3 Behavioural anchors for performance grid

Similarly, the positioning on the grid can be explained in more detail. Figure 4.4 provides this guidance.

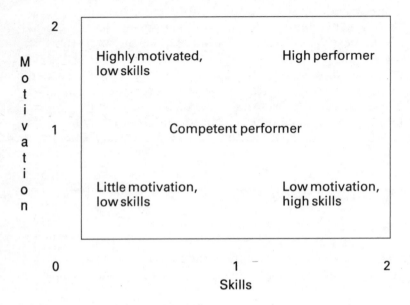

Figure 4.4   Staff's position on the grid

In a 'normal' distribution a large proportion of staff within the work group will cluster around a diagonal on the grid which can be drawn between the top left-hand and bottom right-hand corners. This diagonal represents 'competent performance', and staff being placed on this diagonal may vary between low and high motivation and low and high skills level, but their 'scores' for the assessment on both motivation and skills will add up to 2. For convenience, this summed score is halved so that staff who are assessed as competent and falling along this diagonal have the score of 1 (they can perform the job to 100 per cent of the requirement for that job).

With a small group of 10–20 staff the distribution will not necessarily be 'normal' and clusters of staff may be found in two or three different areas of the grid. It is these 'abnormalities' which can indicate the special characteristics of the group. For example, a cluster of new entrants towards the bottom left-hand corner may indicate not only lack of skills, but also a lack of motivation which may bring into question recruitment and induction policies.

Information collected on the grid can now be transferred to a performance graph (Figure 4.1). The number of staff in each rating category (for example all staff with a rating of 1.5) should be plotted on the graph.

To put a human resource value on the group, it is necessary to calculate the number of each grade of staff performing at an average level for the group (that is, those worth what the organization pays for them: those with a score of 1), and the number of each grade of staff performing at each rating level. The value is the sum of the number of staff per grade (or salary band) with each rating, multiplied by the performance rating, multiplied by the individual value (what persons in each salary band cost the organization) of each grade. This can be expressed as:

Human resource value	=	Number of staff per salary band	×	Cost of staff to organization	×	Performance rating

In other words, we are simply giving each member of staff a 'weighting' according to their value to the organization:

- by their value to the organization in terms of what it is prepared to pay for the services of each member of staff per salary band
- by their level of performance from 0 (no value) through to 1 (100 per cent value: do what they are employed to do) to 2 (200 per cent value: performing well in excess of what they are employed to do).

We are therefore giving an indication of the person's actual value to the organization. Where there are problems, these are 'flagged' in financial terms, as personnel costs money. If they are not performing to the standard required, the deficit to the organization is a real financial one.

Figure 4.5 gives an example of the information which may be obtained using this method.

Figure 4.5 shows performance rating for staff in each grade. For example for grade C staff, two are rated at 2.00, five are rated at 1.75, five at 1.50, and so on. A bar chart is given which shows the total number of staff falling into each rating category: six in 2.00, 16 in 1.75, and so on. The bar chart shows a performance curve peaking at 1.75 and giving a mean performance rating of 1.39. This would indicate that either this work group is performing above what is required of them or the supervisor is lenient in assessing the group. We will see below how we can deal with leniency (page 72). Row 1 gives the total number of staff in each grade or salary band. Row 2 gives the individual personnel value, or the average amount of money each person in each salary band costs the organization. There are several ways of calculating this:

EXAMPLE: PERFORMANCE OF OPERATIONAL SECTIONS FROM SUPERVISOR'S RATINGS

STAFF (BY GRADE).

PERFORMANCE RATING	A	B	C	D	E	F	G	H	
2.00			2	2	1		1		6
1.75		2	5	4	1	1	2	1	16
1.50		4	5	4	2				15
1.25		4	2	3	3	1	1		14
1.00		1	7	2					10
.75		2	2		1				5
.50	1	1							2
.25									0
.00									0

	A	B	C	D	E	F	G	H	
1. Total No. Staff	1	14	23	15	8	2	4	1	68
2. Individual Personnel Value	6092	8327	10300	12166	15423	17375	19448	21629	
3. Current Personnel Value	3046	145723	321875	276777	173509	52125	131274	37851	1142179
4. Nominal Personnel Value (satisfactory performance)	6092	116578	236900	182490	123384	34750	77792	21629	799615
5. Difference From Current Value (Percentage of Current Value)	-3046 50	29145 125	84975 136	94287 152	50125 141	17375 150	53482 169	16222 175	342564 143%
6. Nominal Personnel Value (maximum performance)	12184	233156	473800	364980	246768	69500	155584	43258	1599230
7. Difference From Current Value (Percentage of Current Value)	-9138 25	-87434 63	-151925 68	-88204 76	-73259 70	-17375 75	-24310 84	-5407 88	-457052 71%

Figure 4.5 The value of a work group

- salary plus benefits
- direct personnel costs, which include salary and benefits plus all other direct costs to the organization such as National Insurance and pension contributions
- full absorption cost, including all direct costs plus the costs of all overheads required to keep a member of staff employed, including office accommodation, equipment used, use of secretarial support
- full absorption costs plus contribution to profits, which, when dividing total profits between the number of employees and weighting this for the employee's grade, gives an indication of the value of individuals to the organization by the nominal amount they contribute to profits (see chapter 6 for methods of calculating this).

It does not matter which method is used so long as you are consistent, gain the agreement of the line to the figures used and follow company management accountancy practice.

In Figure 4.5 we have used direct personnel costs. Row 3 gives the current personnel value. For each grade of staff this is arrived at by weighting each individual by the performance rating given. Thus the calculation for staff in grade G would be:

$$[(1 \times 2.00) + (2 \times 1.75) + (1 \times 1.25)] \times £19,448 = £131,274$$
= current personnel value of staff in grade G.

If all staff in grade G perform competently (rating 1.00) their value to the organization will be £77,792 (row 4), the amount that four staff in this grade costs the organization. If we look at row 5 we can see that because they are working above a normal competency level, their value is 169 per cent of competency level or their nominal value (assumed to be 100 per cent value).

However, there is another way of looking at this. Staff can perform at a maximum level (equivalent to rating 2.00). This is a maximum level of attainment if staff have the ability and are trained well. We can therefore assume that anything below this level gives rise to room for improvement: that is, it is possible to improve on a rating of 1.75.

A useful comparison to make is the deficit from this assumed maximum performance. In Figure 4.5, it is possible for grade G staff to have a maximum value to the organization of £155,584 or twice their value at satisfactory performance level. Their actual performance level indicates a value of 84 per cent of the maximum.

The method described above should ideally be combined with self rating. Either the individual member of staff can be asked to place his or her self on the grid, or can discuss with the supervisor where they ought to be placed on the grid, and agreement obtained.

There is often a tendency towards leniency in both supervisor ratings and self ratings of performance (see for example McEnery and McEnery, 1987). Where this is suspected, it may be best to 'float' the performance level at which staff are judged to be performing competently and to be worth what they actually cost the organization, by taking *mean* performance as the competency level. To do this, the mean performance rating is obtained for all staff in the work group. The mean rating is then given the value of the direct personnel cost (or other standard cost which you may be using): that is, this is what the average member of staff is worth to the organization.

The standard deviation is then calculated. For example:

Mean performance rating = 1.50 = £15,000
Standard deviation　　　 = .40 = 　£6,000

Any movement in the mean, following training, can then be calculated in standard deviations: that is, we know a movement of the mean of one standard deviation (or .40) is worth £6,000 or 40 per cent of the value of one member of staff performing at an average level (see for example Cohen and Holliday, 1982, for appropriate statistical calculations).

This method has focused on the use of performance assessment relative to the norms of a work group. Let us now look at a different method of determining the gap in performance, which focuses on criteria of job performance.

DIF (difficulty, importance, frequency) analysis

There are two main aspects of performance criteria development:

- job analysis
- performance assessment.

The method described here is adapted from that used by Cascio and Ramos (1986). DIF (difficulty, importance, frequency) analysis, a relatively well known technique for analysing jobs, is used to give weightings to key functions within a job in order to assign a value to the organization of the tasks and jobs involved. (Cascio and Ramos, 1986, introduce a further concept of consequence of error which has here been combined with importance.)

Criteria for job performance are defined, and an assessment is made on this basis. Each principal job activity is assessed on the basis of the frequency/time devoted to it in terms of percentage of total time, the importance of the activity to overall performance of the operational unit, and the level of difficulty of each activity. Difficulty and importance can be assessed on a four point scale as in Figure 4.6.

Frequency/time involves allocating a percentage of total time to each key activity.

Scale	Difficulty	Importance
1	Easy to learn. Little concentration needed. No knowledge of basic principles.	Of little importance to performance of unit. Errors do not matter.
2	Some practice required to learn and maintain proficiency. Needs concentration. Some grasp of basic principles desirable.	Has some importance to the performance of the unit. Errors may cause inconvenience.
3	Constant practice required. Knowledge of basic principles essential. Decision making required.	Has major importance to performance of unit. Errors and failure to perform adequately may give rise to business or financial loss.
4	Difficult to learn. Experience increases performance. High level of decision making and concentration required. Many factors and concurrent activities.	Unit cannot function without this key activity being competently performed.

Figure 4.6 Criteria for DIF analysis

Suggested criteria for job performance are given in Figure 4.7. This follows the same rating scale as the grid analysis described earlier, but is anchored to criteria of *outcome* rather than *process*.

0	Has produced no results in this function.
0.5	Has produced results in this function which are sometimes (about 50 per cent) consistent with standards of quality and quantity.
1	Has consistently produced results in this function consistent with standards of quality and quantity.
1.5	Has sometimes (about 50 per cent of work) produced results in this function which are well in excess of standards in both quality and quantity.
2	Has consistently produced results in this function well in excess of standards in both quality and quantity.

Figure 4.7 Job performance criteria

Note that this is still *assessment* rather than *measurement* (see pages 59–62) as it is based on supervisor or self ratings which are in turn based on a measure of results. Where possible it should be based on quantifiable criteria of work performance (see Chapter 3). The ratings for each dimension of the principle activities are then multiplied together to give a relative weighting to each activity as in Figure 4.8.

Activity	Difficulty	Importance	Frequency/ Time	Total (D × I × F)	Relative weighting
1.	4	3	30	360	41
2.	2	4	50	400	46
3.	3	3	10	90	10
4.	1	2	5	10	1
5.	4	1	5	20	2
Totals	–	–	100	880	100

Figure 4.8 Example of DIF analysis weightings

The relative weighting for each activity can then be combined with a performance rating obtained from supervisors for each activity.

By using the direct personnel cost of staff a 'value of performance' of each individual can be obtained, as in Figure 4.9.

Activity	Relative weighting	Direct personnel cost £	Value of activity £	Performance rating	Value of performance £
1.	.41	15,000	6,150	1.25	7,688
2.	.46	15,000	6,900	.50	3,450
3.	.10	15,000	1,500	1.00	1,500
4.	.01	15,000	150	2.00	300
5.	.02	15,000	300	1.75	525
Totals	1.00	–	15,000	–	13,463

Figure 4.9 Example calculation for value of performance

This provides a value of performance for one member of staff on supervisor's ratings. The process should be repeated for the whole work group.

Potential performance

Current performance in present job is only one aspect of the value personnel have to the organization. In some ways it is a very shortsighted way of looking at human resources, and an extra dimension is required which projects the value of staff, and the value of training and development, to the future needs of the organization.

Measures of human resource potential are useful to organizations for making decisions about:

- selection
- deployment of staff
- manpower planning
- succession planning
- staff development.

How can we assess potential performance, and how can this be valued? How can we determine the value of development programmes which seek to increase the future value of staff? Grid analysis has already been outlined above, and this general method can be used through a system of *family of grids* to assess potential performance.

Staff are asked to rate themselves on a series of interconnected grids, each along two dimensions beginning with *skills* and *motivation*: the two process factors used before in assessing current performance. Each measure on the grid is verbally anchored to gain standardization of ratings from one member of staff to another. Supervisors are also asked to place each member of their work group on the grids as appropriate, and this is compared with the member of staff's own ratings.

Prediction of potential is based on a number of factors, principally:

- individual's current performance
- ability to develop and do other, more advanced, jobs
- opportunity to progress, which is dependent on operational and corporate objectives, and the type of support and development opportunities available to the individual.

Current performance is an important predictor, but cannot be considered in isolation. Just because individuals perform well in one job does not mean they will perform well in the next. Perhaps more important than actual results achieved in a current job are the 'latent' factors of skills, knowledge and motivation which can be transferred to another job.

Further abilities such as problem solving, decision making, planning, leadership, ability to take on new learning, and adaptability are all indicators of suitability for future advancement in more complex and responsible jobs.

Opportunity and support is the extent to which the individual has the support and encouragement of management in achieving potential, coupled with the suitable supply of opportunities within the organization enabling achievement of potential. Within this factor is the opportunity to gain the right type of training and development.

These factors, when assessed, allow a prediction of *realizable potential:* that is, the potential that may be realized by the individual provided he or she is retained within the organization. However, the *ultimate value* of an individual to the organization is dependent on the probability of retaining that person.

Predictions are made about the future value of human resources in terms of the following factors of individuals:

- promotability
- transferability
- exit from the organization.

These factors provide the measures of potential value of individuals to an organization. The *family of grids* method for assessing these factors is constructed as in Figure 4.10.

Grid no

	Skills/knowledge	Motivation
1	**Current performance**	Further abilities
2	**Potential**	Opportunity/support
3	**Realizable potential**	Direction of career
4	**Ultimate value**	

Figure 4.10 Construction of family of grids: potential performance

The first grid, current performance, asks raters to assess ratees along the two dimensions of motivation and skills/knowledge. The second grid combines current performance with further abilities required to do different jobs at a higher level, to give a picture of potential. The overlapping with the first grid provides a good indication of the reliability of the instrument by checking on the rater's consistency. The third grid stems from the assumption that individuals require the opportunity and support from the line to perform well and realize their potential. This added dimension provides a picture of realizable potential. The fourth grid looks at the ratee's realizable potential against the possibility of his or her leaving the organization, being transferred or gaining promotion *in situ*. This is termed direction of career, and the two dimensions together provide a measure of the person's ultimate value to the organization.

A person who is regarded as a high flier will have a higher ultimate value if there is a probability of retaining that person within the organization. If he or she is likely to leave within a few years, the ultimate value is not so high. Reward packages should be viewed in this light, and development programmes should seek to draw individuals into the organization by providing a connection between individual and corporate objectives: there must be something in it for them; in training and development there should be value for the individual as well as for the organization (this aspect will be explored in Chapter 5).

The value of potential performance, when combined with the value of current performance of individuals, gives a total value of individuals as a human resource. In simple terms, the value of potential performance is the amount an organization is prepared to pay an individual to occupy future roles, against the cost of developing that person, and against the possibility of 'buying in' personnel in each of those roles and the cost of doing so.

Let us look at a hypothetical situation where there are four members of staff currently earning similar salaries. Over the next five years there is the possibility of any of these individuals increasing their salaries by £20,000 up to the maximum grade they would be expected to achieve providing they have the potential. This assumes that they would have the appropriate support and opportunity if they were assessed to have the ability to take advantage of appropriate training and development; if they were not seen as having the ability they would not receive the training and development appropriate to their obtaining the maximum grade.

The company they work for has found that a rating on each grid of the maximum of 2 has indicated a 100 per cent chance of their obtaining that maximum grade in five years, and that obtaining an average rating of 1 on the grids will give them a 50 per cent chance of obtaining this grade. The mean of all ratings on the four grids will therefore provide a 'weighting' if divided by 2 (for example a mean of 2 provides a 100 per cent chance of obtaining the maximum, or equals a weighting of 1.00; a rating of 1 equals a weighting of .50, and so on). This hypothetical case is illustrated in Figure 4.11.

Staff	Current perfor- mance	Potential	Realizable potential	Ultimate value	Mean weight ÷ 2	Maximum increase in value £	Predicted increase in value £
1.	2.0	2.0	2.0	2.0	1	20,000	20,000
2.	1.5	0.5	0.5	0.5	0.38	20,000	20,000
3.	0.5	1.0	0.5	0.5	0.31	20,000	6,200
4.	1.0	0	0	0	0.13	20,000	2,600

Total predicted increase for group	36,400
Average predicted increase for group	9,100

Figure 4.11 Grid analysis: potential performance weightings

Person number 4 in Figure 4.11 was given a rating of nil for the last three predictors, which would seem to indicate no progression past present job. However, the fact that he or she is performing satisfactorily in the present job gives some chance of further progression. On present predictions, the potential value of this individual is £2,600 over current value of performance given a 13 per cent chance of reaching the maximum scale over the next five years. In this situation management may still decide that this person should be provided with training and development opportunities appropriate to attaining the maximum grade. On the other hand, it may be false economy to invest, say, £5,000 in direct costs of training and development for this individual, if the increase in potential value to the organization is not going to exceed this amount.

It may be wiser, and cheaper, to buy in staff with the attributes and skills sought, if sufficient potential cannot be developed in-house.

Another reason for using this method is to indicate the increase in potential value of a work group or an individual after undergoing training intended to develop the skills and attributes their organization seeks when selecting for more complex and responsible jobs.

In this chapter we have looked at ways of assessing and measuring the gap between actual performance and required performance, both current and in the future. In so doing we have concentrated on assessment techniques.

In the next chapter we look at specific methods involving assessment and measurement techniques which seek to determine the value of training and development.

5. Calculating the benefits

Introduction

In this chapter we look at some of the tools for evaluating the benefits of training, and at some of the costs of not training. In Chapter 6 we outline cost-benefit analysis with an emphasis on the costs of training.

Using cost-benefit analysis is not easy. The tools are imperfect, the methods and techniques in their infancy. The foundations for their use has been laid in previous chapters, and they should be used as part of an overall strategy for evaluation.

Methods used must be easy to adapt to different situations, not too complex for the line to understand, and fully acceptable to the line and top management. Similarly, they must stand up to scientific tests of validity. They must be used in practice, tested and finely tuned.

The methods described below follow the same format. Background information is given under 'Description and application'. A brief method is then given as a guide to applying the method in practice. Finally, the relative disadvantages and advantages of using the particular method are given. It is hoped that these methods will provide a starting point for your own applications.

The methods described are as follows:

- *Consequences of not training* is a very simple method which looks at the implications of not training in terms of loss of income to the organization.
- *Performance records* looks at the use of existing performance records in the organization, using turnover of staff as an example of a statistic which many organizations have available.
- *Probability of successful outcome* combines cost-benefit and risk analysis in a method which can be used in calculating the potential success of a training programme, or in deciding between alternative training systems.

- *Costing the learning curve* costs the process of training by looking at the learning curve and comparing different training methods.
- *Action plan audit* suggests a way in which developmental training may be valued.
- *Financial implications of attitudes* applies grid analysis to correlate attitudes with actual behaviour and operational results.

Method: consequences of not training

Description and application

The financial consequences of not training may be serious to an organization. A commercial organization's inability to perform adequately might mean that it is unable to take on additional business, or that it is losing existing business through not being able to cope with the throughput of work.

This very simple method focuses on the actual and potential loss in income to an organization through lack of performance, where the provision of additional and appropriate training may be a factor in increasing performance. A criterion of performance, in this case, is the ability of the organization (or operational unit) to process the income-bearing work in question.

Prior to the 1987 stock market crash, the securities handling market was booming in the City of London, particularly in the light of a succession of privatizations of publicly owned companies by the Conservative government. However, the City was dogged by limited space and a shortage of staff. This meant that rather than the sales revenue being a measure of performance, the ability to process huge volumes of work with limited staff became a measure of performance: ultimately having an effect on the quality of service provided to customers and the ability to take on new business.

Method

1. Establish that there is an actual or potential loss of business. This is most likely within a situation where business within the marketplace is on the increase such as in the example above.

2. Obtain an estimate of what this business is worth, its actual or potential income value, and if possible its value to the organization in terms of profit: for example, it could be unprofitable business or could require additional capital investment which may not be in line with the organization's corporate objectives at this stage of its development. This information is usually forthcoming from the management team.

3. Isolate the factors involved in the lack of performance which may give rise to the loss in business or the inability to take on further business: for example, lack of staff, lack of training, inability to take on staff quickly enough because of lack of training provision, inadequate premises in which to expand (as in the above example), lack of equipment, turnover of staff.

4. If there is more than one factor involved, ascertain the impact of each on the loss of income (see Figure 3.7 for an idea on how to approach this).

5. The full cost of suitable training can be estimated to give a cost-benefit comparison (see Chapter 6 on cost-benefit analysis).

To obtain the above information it is necessary to work with the appropriate line manager and to confirm all data at the highest possible level. The worksheet in Figure 5.1. may help.

Disadvantages

1. Where loss of income (actual or potential) is an issue, the actual amount of loss of income is in some ways an 'accident': that is, it could equally be two thousand pounds worth of business or two billion pounds worth of business. The return on investment (see Chapter 6 for cost-benefit analysis) could therefore be 100 per cent or 2,000,000 per cent!
   This is not really a true measure of the value and effectiveness of training *per se*. It does not give an indication of the increase in value of individual or group performance which could be transposed from one situation to another.

2. It may be difficult to isolate factors involved and to allocate to each their relative weight in relation to income lost. This may depend on the ability of the organization or operational unit to identify this themselves.

3. This method is only applicable to commercial organizations, and usually only in an expanding market.

Advantages

1. Once the potential loss of business is spotted, there is no complex methodology to communicate to the line. The message is simple and straightforward.

2. It is acceptable to the line. Often, the information needed will be volunteered by managers.

Is there business which the company is unable to take on?

. . . .

What is the nature of this business?

. . . .

How much is this business worth (potential £ loss to company)
£ . . . .

Why is the company unable to take this business on?
(rank reasons in number order)

	RANK
Inadequate premises	. . . .
Lack of equipment	. . . .
Lack of staff	. . . .
Inability to take on staff quickly enough	. . . .
High turnover of staff	. . . .
Inadequate training	. . . .
Others	. . . .
- -	. . . .
- -	. . . .

How much more business could be taken on if all existing staff were fully trained? £ . . . .

How much more business could be taken on if new staff could be more quickly trained? £ . . . .

What training would this require?
- -
- -
- -
- -
What would be the cost of this training? £ . . . .

Does the potential increase in business justify the cost of the training?
- -
Potential revenue from increased business £ . . . .
Estimated cost of training £ . . . .

Figure 5.1 Worksheet: the cost of not training

This method can be adapted to suit the organization or operational unit. For example, the consequences of not training could equally be measured by:

- loss of output
- loss of time
- loss of quality
- increase in costs.

The point is that it costs money not to train and develop staff, and, rather than being a cost saving to reduce the training budget, it may well lead to a loss of revenue and an increase in organizational costs.

Method: performance records

Description and application

Where possible, existing performance records should be used to determine pre-training and post-training performance. This will save time in collecting data and will more easily gain the commitment of the line. Different performance records will be found appropriate in different situations.

Method

1. Identify, with the appropriate line manager, where existing performance problems are and what records are available to confirm these problems. The checklist in Figure 5.2 will help. (See also Phillips, 1983, page 89, and refer to Chapter 3 of the current text.)

2. An initial survey of performance records will help in establishing training needs, and in setting objectives for training (see Chapters 2 and 3).

3. Appropriate records should be identified which provide measurable information on performance prior to training, which are related to the pre-stated course objectives, and which are capable of indicating any change in performance as a result of training.

4. The cost of any performance deficiencies should be calculated, alongside the investment in training needed to provide a cost-benefit analysis (see Chapter 6).

The following serves as an example, where it is possible to isolate a lack of training as a factor contributing to turnover of staff.

The cost of staff turnover

The costs of staff turnover are both outlay costs and time costs. Figure 5.3 is a checklist of costs for entry and exit of staff which should be taken into consideration and costed accordingly.

Add up all outlay and time costs to give the total cost of turnover of one employee. Multiply the number of staff replaced this year to give total costs of turnover of staff.

Record of:	Available in this ✓ organization?	Where available?
Absenteeism		
Budget variance		
Costs		
Customer complaints		
Employees promoted		
Errors		
Grievances		
Lateness		
Machine downtime		
New business		
Output		
Percentage of quota achieved		
Rejection of work		
Sales		
Targets met		
Turnover of staff		
Work backlog		
Others		

Figure 5.2 Checklist of performance records

	Costs	
	Outlay £	Time £
Entry		
Preparation of job description		
Advertising		
Communicating with agencies		
Agency fees		
Shortlisting		
Pre-interview administration		
Administration of selection tests		
Interviews		
Travel and expenses		
Selection decision meetings		
Notification of decision		
Other associated administration		
Medicals		
Post-employment administration		
Relocation/temporary accommodation		
Induction		
Other initial training		
Learning curve (lack of productivity)		
Exit		
Counselling/disciplinary meetings		
Documenting performance problems		
Termination meetings		
Other administration (eg salaries)		
Lost productivity during separation period		
Cost of vacant position		
Individual total × number of employees replaced this year		
TOTAL COST OF TURNOVER		

(Adapted from Spencer, 1986, pages 118–21)

Figure 5.3 Cost of staff replacement

Disadvantages

1. Appropriate performance records are sometimes not available. Sometimes line managers are reluctant to give performance data which, they think, may reflect badly on them.

2. Performance records often do not give enough information to measure pre- and post-training performance.

Advantages

1. Existing records are readily acceptable to the line as an indication of performance.

2. Existing performance records save work for the training function in developing measures.

Method: probability of successful outcome

Description and application

This method looks at the process of training. By using cost-benefit methods and risk analysis, it assesses the value of inputs (costs) into the process, and the value of outputs (benefits) from the process. It is a useful method where there is a need to make decisions about alternative training systems, or where it is appropriate to calculate the potential or actual success of a training programme.

Method

1. Identify the 'system' of training (see Figure 5.4).

2. Calculate inputs. All inputs to be costed (*process* costs), and the lack of value of trainees to be calculated as a cost (*outcome* cost). For example, a new trainee with nil knowledge and experience, and costing the organization £10,000 in personnel costs represents an annual deficit in value of £10,000 until fully competent to do the job (see also pages 89–90, 'Costing the Learning Curve').

3. Define criteria for outputs. For example a 'competent' member of staff to be defined by the accepted standards of work of an experienced person.

4. Value a 'competent' member of staff by reference to personnel costs multiplied by the average time spent in the post of an experienced job holder.

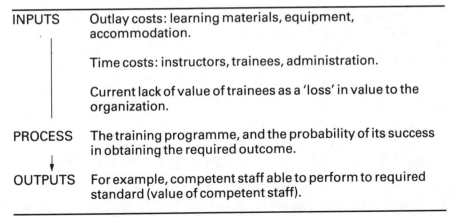

INPUTS   Outlay costs: learning materials, equipment, accommodation.

               Time costs: instructors, trainees, administration.

               Current lack of value of trainees as a 'loss' in value to the organization.

PROCESS   The training programme, and the probability of its success in obtaining the required outcome.

OUTPUTS   For example, competent staff able to perform to required standard (value of competent staff).

Figure 5.4 Training system

5. Assess the process. Calculate the probability of success of the training system. The easiest way of doing this is by using risk analysis (see Armstrong, 1986) as in the example in Figure 5.5.

Example

Level of competency after course %	Value of staff after course £	Likelihood of achieving level of competency %	Expected value of outcome £
0	0	0	0
25	2,500	25	625
50	5,000	25	1,250
75	7,500	25	1,875
100	10,000	25	2,500
	Totals	100%	£6,250

Figure 5.5 Risk analysis (expected value technique)

The 'level of competency after course' column represents five different levels after completion of a course from 0 per cent competency to 100 per cent. If individuals are valued by their cost to the organization (in this case £10,000) then the 'value of staff after course' weights this by the competency level shown in column one. The likelihood of achieving each of these levels is shown in the column 'Likelihood of achieving level of competency' as being equal for 25, 50, 75, 100 per cent, while there is no chance of having a nil competency level. The likelihood of achieving a level of competency as a result of the course is calculated on a sample of ex-participants.

Finally, the 'expected value of outcome' is determined by calculating the percentage of each value: there is a 25 per cent chance of staff being worth £2,500; a 25 per cent chance of staff being worth £5,000, and so on. On this basis, the total expected value of an individual after completing this course is £6,250. Obviously the course is not totally effective.

6. Subtract all inputs (costs) from outputs (benefits) to give net benefits of the process (the course).

If required, calculate the return on investment as a ratio of costs/benefits (see Chapter 6).

7. If appropriate, compare with other training systems or methods such as on-the-job training.

It could be appropriate to collect information on the length of time taken to complete training, particularly when considering on-the-job training as compared with a course or other structured approach. This would figure as a cost and lack of value in the untrained person.

Instead of a percentage competency, have a pass/fail situation where the trainee either reaches the standard or does not. Time would then be a factor in this as a major cost would be the time taken to train to a 'competent' level. Then calculate the probability aspect as in (5.) above.

Disadvantages

1. It is sometimes difficult to obtain objective and standardized criteria of performance. A particular problem may be in obtaining measures of individuals' competency across a national organization with operational units engaged in the same activities. This problem occurs in the finance industry where individuals' performances are not necessarily related to sales, and may relate to a clerical function: performance may be differently conceived by numerous different managers.

A method to counter variation in criteria is to take a wide sample of branches or local offices, average out criteria, incorporate these within *outcome* objectives for the training course, and communicate these objectives to the various branch managers to obtain agreement. Criteria are then met if objectives of the training programme are met.

2. With existing training programmes, objectives are not always clearly defined in tems of the expected outcome of the training, in line with

performance criteria. This should not be a problem if the process described in Chapters 2 and 3 is followed.

3. The method may appear complicated. It needs to be clearly communicated to the line.

Advantages

1. This method provides a good basis for predicting the value of the outcome of training programmes.

2. It provides a means of comparing one training 'system' with another. The information so obtained can be used to make decisions about the cost-effectiveness of different types of training provision.

Method: costing the learning curve

Description and application

In choosing between different methods of training, the speed at which a person becomes fully competent in the job is a good indicator of their relative success. This method costs the learning curve by measuring the time it takes a person from nil knowledge and experience to become competent in the job.

Method

1. Develop criteria for a fully 'competent' member of staff by reference to what that person should be able to do, and to what standard.

2. During and following training, document the individual's performance along a learning curve as illustrated in Figure 5.6.
   This can be undertaken by using supervisor's ratings based on pre-determined performance criteria for 25, 50, 75 and 100 per cent competency or on existing performance data.

3. The shaded area of the graph in Figure 5.6, the non-productive area, should be costed in terms of shortfall in the value of the individual to the organization.

4. Alternative methods of training can be compared to find the most cost-effective (see Chapter 6 for a definition of 'cost-effectiveness').

5. Any 'saving' made through decreasing the unproductive area on the graph through using a different training method, is a benefit of the new training method (see for example Spencer, 1986).

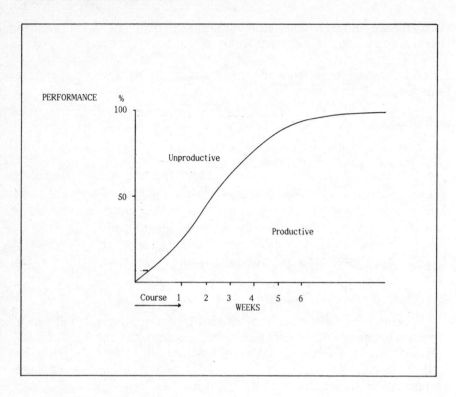

Figure 5.6 A learning curve

Disadvantages

The use of supervisor or trainee ratings retrospectively should be avoided. Performance data should be documented at the end of each agreed period, for example each week. This may be onerous.

Advantages

This is an effective method for comparing courses and different methods of training.

Method: action plan audit

Description and application

By course participants putting a plan into action to improve performance following the course, a management training and development course can be valued in terms of benefits to the organization.

The action plan can be audited to measure results.

The best way to achieve results back at the workplace following a training course is to plan for it, develop the necessary skills within the course, discuss the plan during the course to develop the best way to implement it, and put it into practice once back on the job. Results can then be monitored in line with expectations (see for example Phillips, 1983).

Method

1. During the course a plan can be drawn up by course participants for action to be taken on the job, in order to use the new skills and knowledge acquired and, indeed, as a focus for developing skills in the classroom. The plan should include:

- clearly stated objectives which indicate the purpose of the action including operational improvements and benefits in financial terms

Example
A subject for a supervisory skills course could be 'to increase productivity on my section by a 50 per cent increase in the speed of handling claim forms to clear the backlog of post, and to decrease complaints by 75 per cent; this would give a 50 per cent increase in the human resource value of the section, and would reduce the closure of accounts by an estimated 25 per cent (all these targets being measurable in financial terms)'.

- a programme of enabling objectives and steps to take to achieve those objectives (*enabling* objectives are objectives in each stage which enable the achievement of the final objective or goal)
- a timescale for each step of the action programme, and a deadline to achieve the overall objectives.

2. The plan should be implemented by course participants, a record being kept of action taken and objectives achieved.

3. The record of the action programme should be audited by the training team, in cooperation with the participants' supervisor, to reveal the objectives achieved and the value to the organization of those achievements (see for example Phillips, 1983).

Disadvantages

Course participants may find it difficult to identify problem areas to be addressed by this type of action planning. They may find it difficult to attach a cash benefit to their achievements if they are not given help in this.

However, participants and their supervisors should have identified problems and needs before attending the course, and pre-course material should be provided for this purpose. Assessing benefits in financial terms should be an integral part of the course.

Advantages

This method is directly related to the training course, the trainer requires little pre-training performance data, and the method encourages results-orientated training.

Calculating the benefits to individuals

So far in this text we have concentrated on the benefits of training and development to the organization. One of the most important functions of training and development is to bring individual and organizational objectives closer together. If individuals within the organization see that their own objectives, in terms of their working and family life, and their career aspirations, do not coincide with the way they see their jobs in the organization, either the individual and organization will part company, or there will be dissatisfied people working in the organization.

We concentrate here on attitudes, as being important for both individual and organization. An attitude is an internal state of mind which contains within it a predisposition to act. People can choose whether they will do something or not. They can choose the amount of effort they will put into performing a particular task or job. This will depend on their attitudes to themselves, the tasks involved, other people, and the organization in which they work.

These attitudes might be:

- towards self: self confidence, drive, ambition
- towards tasks: intrinsic motivation, interest
- towards other people: respect, attraction
- towards the organization: involvement, identification, satisfaction with opportunities.

To put this into perspective, the level of performance within an organization results from a combination of three interrelated factors, as shown in Figure 5.7.

Conduct is the way we act, what we do, and is largely dependent on the level of skills we have to do a job. This is the factor that training largely addresses: that is, the acquisition and improvement of skills to do the job.

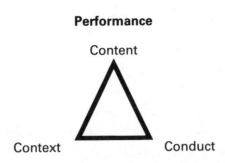

Figure 5.7 Performance factors

Context is the organizational factor and includes the organizational structure, systems and technology employed. This has implications for the nature of the work and the opportunities within the organization.

Content is the way people see their world, themselves, their jobs, the people they work with. The stems from 'self concept' – the way individuals see and evaluate themselves and their world – and interacts with conduct (behaviour) and context (the opportunities available within the work environment).

Content comprises attitudes to conduct and context (and draws attitudes from these two other factors) and has fundamental implications for performance and training.

Attitudes are therefore a major factor in performance improvement (and therefore training and development) and can be affected by: skills training, by building the skills, and therefore confidence, to do the job; by specific strategies for building motivation and self concept; and by building the organizational opportunities. Attitudes are identifiable and their implications measurable. They have implications for improved performance which can be evaluated in terms of financial implications for the organization.

A *family of grids* approach (see Chapter 4) can be used to assess attitudes. The 'family' of attitudes which we are assessing are set out diagrammatically in Figure 5.8.

From Figure 5.8 we can obtain two grids, one for 'performance in job' comprising 'attitude to task' and 'attitude to self', and one for 'opportunity and environment' comprising 'attitude to others' and

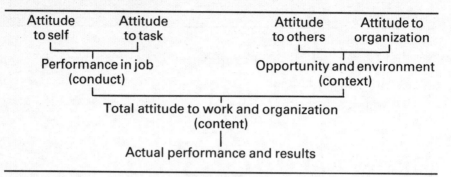

Figure 5.8 'Family' of attitudes

'attitude to organization'. These grids can be verbally anchored, and Figure 5.9 is a suggestion for verbal anchors for the 'Performance in Job' grid for completion by the supervisor.

Performance in job

Attitudes to self (self-confidence, drive, ambition)

0   Has no self-confidence, drive or ambition
0.5   Requires more self-confidence to do the job, and more ambition to get on in the organization
1.0   Has sufficient self-confidence to do a competent job. May progress through own ambition
1.5   Has a certain self-confidence, drive and ambition which is shown much of the time
2.0   Has a great deal of self-confidence, drive and ambition which is shown all the time

Attitude to task/job (motivated by present job)

0   Is not motivated by current job
0.5   Is motivated a little by current job which sometimes provides a small degree of satisfaction
1.0   Derives a moderate amount of satisfaction from current job which motivates from time to time
1.5   Mostly motivated by current job which often provides satisfaction
2.0   Current job motivates very highly and provides a high degree of satisfaction most of the time

Figure 5.9 Verbal anchors for 'performance in job' grid

Similar verbal anchors can be constructed for the other grid, and for grids for completion by the individuals themselves. Staff and supervisors rate staff on each grid according to the two dimensions on the grid. Ratings can be summed and averaged to give an overall attitude rating as in Figure 5.10.

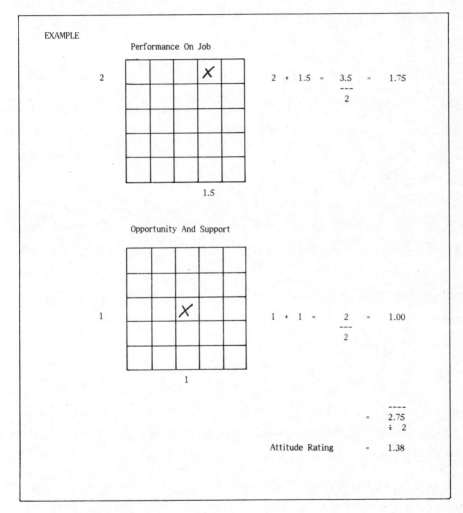

Figure 5.10 Attitude ratings

At this stage the attitude rating is merely a useful comparison of attitudes between staff, work groups and over time.

Attitude scores can only be seen to have financial implications when correlated with actual behaviour and results. Specifically, these can be:

- voluntary turnover of staff
- absenteeism (uncertified, short-term illness)
- lateness
- reported errors.

These behavioural 'results' of attitudes can be costed and correlated with attitude ratings as in Figure 5.11.

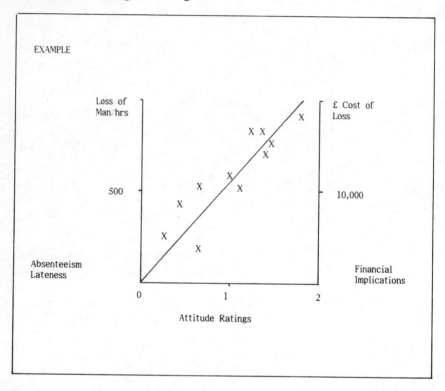

Figure 5.11 Correlation of attitude ratings and behavioural implications

Cascio (1982) provides research evidence to suggest a positive correlation between attitudes such as lack of work satisfaction and absenteeism, and the example in Figure 5.11 shows a pattern which may emerge if these two are compared. This is useful in predicting results following changes in attitude brought about by specific training and development programmes and organizational development. Cascio (1982) suggests a positive correlation between attitudes measured and behaviour/results three months later, and this should be borne in mind when applying the above methods.

We have in this chapter explored various methods of calculating benefits of training and development, and looked at various facets of human behaviour in organizations. In the next chapter we will bring everything together by considering cost-benefit analysis and its position within the strategic framework painted in Chapters 1 to 3, and consider how evaluation can be developed within organizations.

6. Putting it all together

Cost-benefit analysis

This chapter provides a synthesis or pulling together of the ideas and information presented so far, to point the way forward for evaluating training and development in your own organization.

You will have noticed that much of the background information given, and the slant of this text, is towards a commercial service industry and towards 'intangible' skills of management and human relations rather than, for example, a production industry and operator or technical skills. This reflects the industry in which the present author works, and his particular training and development interests. It is probably more difficult to evaluate training in these areas than in, for example, production or sales. Many of the strategies and techniques suggested in this text apply equally in other industries and in other training areas: in many ways it is easier to apply the basic model developed in Chapters 2 and 3 in production or sales.

Non-commercial sectors are becoming increasingly interested in evaluating training and development. Health authorities and local government authorities have a need to make limited resources as effective as possible. Trainers need to show a contribution to cost-effectiveness. Benefits cannot always be shown in financial terms in these industries, other than in cost savings. Benefits are not related to profit, but are related to the improved service provided to clients. Similarly, in commercial organizations as well as non-profit organizations, not all benefits are financially related, but relate to the benefits to individuals and to the community within which those individuals and the particular industry exist.

Cost-benefit, strictly, is about all costs and all benefits: costs and benefits in human terms as well as in financial terms. Social, economic and behavioural sciences (the disciplines which have been applied in this text) should not lose sight of those individuals who are so often referred to as 'human resources'. The reason why we have not concentrated on this 'human' (rather than the 'resource') aspect, is not because it is unimportant, but because the objective of this book is to show how human behaviour within a business situation, can be converted to and measured in financial terms: human beings are an important resource to business and other organizations, they have value in financial terms; their value can be increased; without valuable human beings, organizations do not work.

Let us begin at the beginning and look at cost-benefit analysis and what it means. We can first contrast *cost-benefit* with *cost-effectiveness analysis* as these two terms are sometimes confused. Definitions are simply stated by Armstrong (1986), as follows.

> Cost-effectiveness analysis compares alternative courses of action in terms of their costs and their effectiveness in attaining some specific objective.
> Cost-benefit analysis conducts a monetary assessment of the total costs and revenues or benefits of a project, paying particular attention to the social costs and benefits which do not normally feature in conventional costing exercises.
> (Armstrong, 1986, pages 344–9)

Cost-effectiveness focuses on choices, given common objectives, and seeks an alternative which will give good value for money, provided it achieves the desired end.

Much of what is covered in this text could be evaluated solely in cost-effectiveness terms, given pre-stated objectives for a training programme. Other methods of delivering that programme could be evaluated (see methods described in Chapter 5).

In cost-benefit analysis we are interested in all benefits accruing as a result of instigating a training programme. These include benefits to:

- the individual undergoing the programme
- that person's immediate work group or team
- the operational unit or department within which that person works
- the organization
- the community within which the above exist.

As an example, if a person is well trained as a manager, that should give benefits to his or her work group, operating unit and organization in financial terms. In addition the work group may better enjoy working under a good manager and satisfaction with work may increase. This has benefits to the organization in financial terms as we have seen in Chapter 5, and has personal benefits to the individuals concerned in terms of less stress and a happier work life. Trained managers may also benefit in terms of gaining work satisfaction and increasing their earning potential.

Let us look at this from the community's point of view. There are now within the industrial community trained managers who may work equally well or better for another company. This is a benefit to the managers as they may be able to get another job at a higher salary; it is also a benefit to the industry as there are fewer managers to train, and more managers who can be bought in. This may seem not to be good for the company who trained the manager: they may lose the cost of training and the trained manager as well (see the discussion on 'ultimate value' of personnel in Chapter 4). However, if other companies are training managers just as well, and if these trained managers are equally available on the job market, then our company in this example is not really losing – simply adding to the existing pool of trained managers in the industry from which they can pick and choose.

Cost-benefit analysis therefore has wider implications which should perhaps be considered before the implementation of training and development programmes. Let us now look at how cost-benefit analysis fits in with the methodologies outlined in this text.

We have said that the training and development process involves a system of inputs and outputs (pages 44–45), and that inputs are generally costs to the system and outputs are generally benefits. Outputs can also be negative and detrimental to the organization. Let us say that we develop managers and raise in them expectations which cannot be immediately satisfied in their current jobs. They may leave for other organizations which can satisfy that new level of expectation. This would constitute a cost, as we have seen above.

Costs can therefore be of two types:

- input costs (expenditure)
- output costs (losses).

Let us look at the input costs of training.

The stages of training are represented in the training model presented in Figure 1.1. This is the process we must cost in terms of the input into it. For each stage in the training process, costs are incurred as follows.

Expenses:
- travel
- food, living accommodation
- materials per student
- services purchased (eg consultant)
- equipment hired
- room hire.

Personnel costs:
- direct personnel cost per in-house trainer.

Overhead costs:
- accommodation occupancy costs
- support staff
- legal, insurance and other costs
- downtime of trainees.

Opportunity costs:
- Sales, production or other losses as a result of trainees attending a course, line managers giving advice, etc.

By employing absorption costing methods, overhead and opportunity costs can be apportioned to personnel costs of both trainers and trainees as follows.

Cost of in-house trainer:
- direct personnel costs (salary, benefits, National Insurance, pension contributions and other direct costs of employing that person)
- apportionment of full cost of support staff
- apportionment of office space and equipment used.

Cost of releasing trainee or line manager for consultation:
- direct personnel costs
- apportionment of full cost of any support staff
- apportionment of contribution to operational results (eg sales, production, etc).

Calculating the cost of releasing personnel to attend a course or help develop training is important as it shows the loss of value in staff during absences. The benefits must outweigh the loss in production or sales that may result.

The above costs should be allocated to each stage in the training process outlined in Figure 1.1, namely:

Stage:
1. identify training needs
2. analyse training needs
3. write training objectives
4. develop programme
5. conduct programme
6. evaluate programme
7. communicate results.

Figure 6.1 gives a worksheet for calculating costs on the basis suggested above.

COSTS Stage	1	2	3	4	5	6	7	Totals
00 Trainers (absorption)								
01 Line managers (absorption)								
02 Trainees (absorption)								
03 Room hire								
04 Equipment hire								
05 Purchased services								
06 Purchased materials								
07 In-house reproduction								
08 Trainers' expenses								
09 Line managers' expenses								
10 Trainees' expenses								
Totals								

Figure 6.1 Costing worksheet

Trainers' time is calculated on a daily basis. For an in-company trainer it is worth thinking of this in terms of 'billable' time. If this trainer's services were provided to outside organizations, how much would have to be charged to break even? The calculation would look something like this:

 Salary
+ Benefits
+ National Insurance contributions
+ Superannuation
+ Other direct costs incurred by employer

+ Percentage use of support staff (apportionment of their absorption costs)
+ Percentage of overheads (apportionment of total overheads including accommodation rent, utilities, rates, upkeep, etc, and equipment used)

÷ Number of days worked per year
× Number of days spent on each stage of the training process.

For line managers who may be helping to develop a programme, or for those course participants who need to leave their place of work to attend a course, an extra cost may be incurred through a loss in production or sales, or the need to employ a 'margin' of staff to cover such absences. This 'opportunity' cost may be calculated in a number of ways: for example, the contribution to profit of each person may be used. This is calculated simply by dividing the total profit by the number of staff. Weights may be given for the salary band in which each group of staff falls representing a different contribution to profits.

These are the input costs of training: those that need to be incurred to develop and execute the training programme. Output costs are the negative results which may accrue following the programme. Staff might leave the organization for a better-paid job elsewhere if they find that they are more marketable as a result of enhanced skills and knowledge. Certain courses which assess individuals may demotivate individuals if they are seen to do badly in the assessment. Benefits resulting should be compared to total costs to give a cost-benefit comparison.

Cost-benefit analysis may be undertaken before beginning a project, based on estimates, to make a decision on whether to proceed, or may be undertaken after the event to assess whether a programme is worth while. It may be stated in terms of a return on investment: what does the organization get for its investment (input costs) in training? This can be expressed in terms of a return-on-investment ratio, as follows:

$$\text{Return on investment} = \frac{\text{Benefits of programme}}{\text{Input cost (investment)}}$$

This is information which should be used by trainers to communicate total benefits to the line and senior management, and by line managers to make a judgement on the suitability of training as a management tool, compared to other management tools which may be appropriate.

We have therefore put the benefits of training and development in the context of the costs, or investment into training, but have not spent too much time on this aspect as it is covered well elsewhere (notably Spencer, 1986). In fact, the cost of training is an area that may have a high profile in organizations, to the detriment of the training department: costs should be shown in relation to the benefits accruing from training and development – that is, as an investment. This subject has therefore been left for the last chapter of this book, rather than dealt with at the beginning which is often the case in other texts.

The results-orientated model presented in Figure 1.1, together with the 'business model' given in Figure 1.4, and developed extensively throughout Chapter 2 and 3, make a powerful strategic approach to evaluation. We now turn to the integration of these two models to see how they combine together to form a complete 'results-orientated business model for training.'

A results-orientated business model for training

To explain the principle behind this model it is a good idea to consider the way in which social behaviour may be scientifically studied. This involves a debate which goes back to the advent of social science: can social behaviour be studied scientifically and, if so, how?

The main arguments against social behaviour being scientifically studied are that there are too many factors involved in human behaviour and that these cannot possibly be isolated to provide us with an objective answer to what causes what, or a cause and effect explanation; and that we, as human beings, are too involved in the process of human relations to stand back and assess behaviour objectively.

The problem in evaluation, as in social explanation, is that the exploration is very often attempted after the event. Once a social event takes place, such as a training programme, an attempt is made to provide an explanation in terms of its causes and effects: that is, what effects this training programme has had on the individuals attending it and on the organization in which they work.

A body of theory has been built up over the years in the social sciences which, the current author believes, closest fits what happens in everyday life. This very practical theory has been called by various names including 'social analysis' (Rowbottom, 1977) and, more aptly, 'action research' (see for example Cohen and Manion, 1980). The approach taken is that an intervention is made within a social system with particular objectives. The scientific test of cause and effect is whether the intervention made brings about the desired effect: that is, is the intervention *valid*? This is a rather simplistic way of explaining the approach, but it reflects 'common sense' which says that if you set out to achieve something, and you actually achieve it, most of the things you did to get there must have been right.

The approach taken in this text is just that: first looking at what the organization's policy makers are trying to achieve, and perhaps helping them to clarify ideas and strategy; then looking at how they are trying to achieve objectives by operational means, and what needs to be done to ensure the individuals in the organization can achieve operational objectives by developing appropriate skills; and finally focusing on the achievement of objectives to see if these have been achieved on the basis of the actions taken.

Training and development is an intervention in social life. It is made in order to affect behaviour in a particular way. That particular way is planned before the event and objectives with definite targets are set out beforehand. Either these targets are achieved, or they are not. If they are achieved we can assume that our intervention has had the desired effect; it is thus validated.

By using the strategy described in Chapters 2 and 3 it is very difficult for a trainer to be just a trainer. By adopting a strategy which focuses on improving performance in line with corporate objectives, he or she has to be aware of:

- the marketplace or environment in which the organization operates
- strategic decisions taken which impact on operational objectives
- the operating situation from the point of view of the line, whose main concern is not training but improving performance and demonstrating that performance has been improved
- individual performance and how it can be improved by developing skills.

The trainer needs to be:

- a business man or woman (first and foremost in a business environment) who understands the direction in which performance must be driven and stated in financial terms
- someone who understands organizational analysis and development

- a specialist in performance analysis and development
- a behavioural specialist who can analyse skills and develop them.

To see how this all fits into place let us return to our original business model outlined in Figure 1.4, 'A model for evaluation design', and develop it a stage further (Figure 6.2).

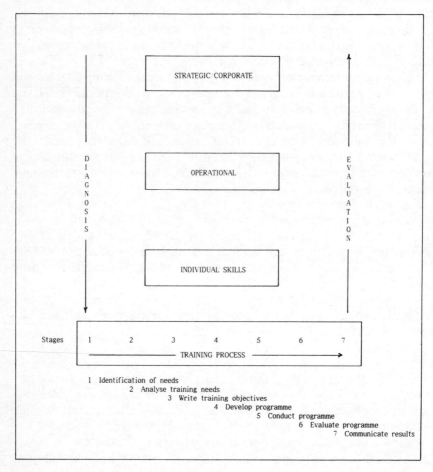

Figure 6.2 A results-orientated business model

Interventions can be made at any stage within the process model in Figure 6.2 to improve performance. At the strategic level, strategic planning can be sharpened, and trainers may intervene by providing assistance in developing the skills of strategic thinking, planning and organizational development, as well as by changing management at a senior level. Direct inteventions may also need to be made by using methods other than training to facilitate corporate cultural change, structural change or employee communication.

At an operational level, line managers may need to be trained to manage performance of existing resources or to initiate and follow through specific projects for improving performance and introducing new resources, possibly drawing on non-line project managers and outside help. Organizational development interventions at this level may include the development of work teams.

The skills level is really the domain of the trainer *per se,* and this includes the training mentioned above for strategic planning and for operational performance improvement. These interventions are shown diagrammatically in Figure 6.3.

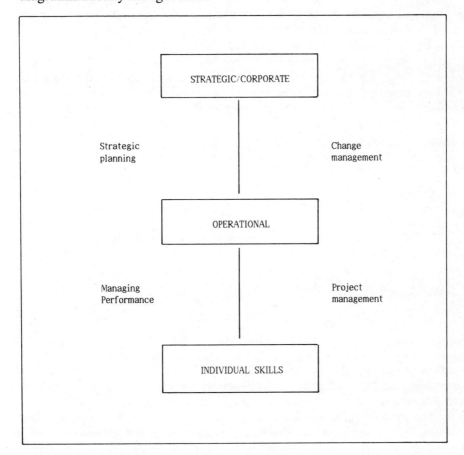

Figure 6.3 Interventions in the business model

This text has concentrated on the intervention at skills level – training (Figure 6.2) – but this is complementary to the intervention at the other two levels in the model in Figure 6.3. The same diagnostic/evaluation 'loop' applies and this was explained in Chapters 2 and 3. By following through this loop, any intervention is results orientated, and the test of a successful intervention is that is gives the results defined by the diagnostic phase.

Once a need is identified by senior or line managers (stage 1 in the training process), training and development needs are analysed by looking at corporate, operational and skills levels. This ensures that training objectives are aligned with strategic requirements, results of which are ultimately defined in financial terms (stage 3). The programme is designed (stage 4) and the intervention made (stage 5). Data is collected at all levels, skills, operational and corporate, and compared with base-line data collected prior to the intervention. This is then communicated to the line and senior management, and is used as a basis for management decision making (see Figure 6.2).

This process is costed as explained above (see Figure 6.1) and benefits arising from the process are compared to objectives and specific targets set prior to the training intervention. The main benefit arising as a result of training and development is the closing of the performance gap, as we discussed in Chapter 4. Where possible, this gap should be *measured* on specific outputs before and after the intervention, and the difference compared. Alternatively, or in addition, the gap may be *assessed* and related to the value of human resources. Any increase in value is a benefit of the intervention.

Any benefit over and above the costs of the intervention is a positive return on investment in training and development. Both costs and benefits must be shown in comparable units such as £s. Interventions made at any other level in this model may also be evaluated in this way, by showing a direct benefit which relates to corporate objectives.

Selling evaluation

It is impossible to sell evaluation. The old sales adage that you cannot sell a product, you can only sell its benefits is true here but inadequate as a statement of the problems of selling evaluation in an organization. You can only sell training and development, or at least the benefits of training and development. Evaluation shows the value of such an intervention.

Having said that, you will still have to convince the organization of the desirability of spending money on evaluation, particularly if training and development is seen as important and the organization is willing to spend money on it. The main problem you will have will probably be with other trainers who do not want to have their work evaluated, and you will need a certain amount of tenacity to win through.

What are the arguments for evaluation?

1. If you made a significant investment (say £1 million) in a business would you not expect to see a return on this investment? Would you not want to account for every penny, to see that it was being used wisely, and that the maximum return possible was being obtained from it? If the answer is yes, then why should training and development be immune from normal business practice?

2. If you do not assess the effects of what you are doing, how do you know you are doing the right things? Just because your course participants are giving you high ratings does not mean that you are developing skills, that these skills are being applied in the workplace, and that they are having an impact on operational and corporate results. Training's entertainment value does not equal its value to the organization! If you evaluate what you are doing properly you can ensure you are being effective. If you are not, you can change the training intervention to make sure your work is of value to the organization.

3. Has your chief executive ever asked what contribution the training and development function is making? If not, there will come a time when this question is asked, probably when cost cutting is necessary. Can you show that it is false economy to cut your training budget?

4. Are you paid as much as your colleagues in other functions, such as marketing, production or finance? Are you regarded on a par with them? If not, have you ever asked yourself why? It is the job of professionals to show the worth of their function. Are you being professional in your approach to the business of your organization?

This may convince you, but how do you convince others in your organization?

1. Work with the line to develop measures which are acceptable and will show an increase in performance for the line manager.
2. Make sure that your training programmes are in line with corporate and operational objectives and that they do yield results for the line managers (the results are theirs, not yours). Then let line management argue the case for you.
3. Communicate measurable results achieved to the highest level; make sure they are well publicized.

4. Demonstrate the purpose of this information, what it can be used for, and its implications for human resourcing decisions, budgeting and planning, and making best use of people's time; and particularly in showing a return on the investment made in training and development.

Remember that evaluation is not something that is done in isolation: it is a complete approach to training and development, as it is to organizational development and to strategic planning.

In summary, in this text we have discussed a business-orientated approach to training and development, with evaluation integral to this.

Sometimes, the term 'evaluation' seems insufficient to encompass the range covered by this expression. Sometimes human resource people become very defensive when this word is bandied around. It is really quite a harmless little word which means, as this book has suggested, 'ensuring value for the organization in business terms'. As such it is a very powerful concept because of the things trainers have to do to ensure value. They have to understand the business objectives of the organization and line up with these objectives what they do in the training room and in the operational units. They have to ensure that they get results which help the organization achieve corporate objectives. Further, they need to understand the language of business. They need to speak in pounds and pence. Investments in business are made in cash; a financial return is expected.

Evaluation, therefore, is about relating training to business performance. If training cannot be related to the performance of the organization, it is probably a waste of time and certainly a waste of money!

References

Argyle, M (1967) *The Psychology of Interpersonal Behaviour,* Harmondsworth: Penguin

Armstrong, M (1986) *A Handbook of Management Techniques,* London: Kogan Page

Berliner, D C, Angell, D and Shearer, J W (1964) 'Behaviours, Measures, and Instruments for Performance Evaluation in Simulated Environments', quoted in Fleishman, E A and Quaintaince, M K (1984) *Taxonomy of Human Performance,* New York: Academic Press

Blake, R R and Mouton, J S (1978) *The New Management Grid,* Houston: Gulf Publishing

Brogden, H E (1949) 'When Testing Pays Off', in *Personnel Psychology,* Vol 33

Burns, R B (1979) *The Self Concept,* London: Longman

Cascio, W F (1982) *Costing Human Resources,* New York: Van Nostrand Reinhold

Cascio, W F and Ramos, R A (1986) 'Development and Application of a New Method for Assessing Job Performance in Behavioural/ Economic Terms', *Journal of Applied Psychology,* vol 71, No 1, pages 20–8

Cohen, L and Holliday, M (1982) *Statistics For the Social Scientist,* London: Harper and Row

Cohen, L and Manion, L (1980) *Research Methods in Education,* London: Croom Helm

Coonradt, C A (1985) *The Game of Work,* Salt Lake City: Shadow Mountain

Crosby, P B (1979) *Quality Is Free: The Art of Making Quality Certain,* New York: Mentor/McGraw-Hill

Flamholtz, E (1974) *Human Resource Accounting,* California: Dickenson

Ford, J K and Noe, R A (1987) 'Self-Assessed Training Needs: The Effects of Attitudes Towards Training, Managerial Level, and Function', in *Personnel Psychology,* Vol 40, pages 39–53

Gannon, M J (1982) *Management: An Integrated Approach,* Boston: Little, Brown and Co

Goldstein, I L (1986) *Training in Organizations: Needs Assessment, Development and Evaluation,* California: Brooks/Cole

Greiner, L E and Metzger, R O (1983) *Consulting To Management,* New Jersey: Prentice-Hall

Jackson, T (1989) *Fifty Activities for Improving Interpersonal Communication,* Aldershot: Gower

Katz, D and Kahn, R L (1978) *The Social Psychology of Organizations,* New York: John Wiley

Kubr, M [Ed] (1980) *Management Consulting: A Guide to the Profession,* Geneva: International Labour Office

Leavitt, H J (1951) 'Some Effects of Certain Communication Patterns on Group Performance', in *Journal of Abnormal and Social Psychology,* Vol 46, pages 38–50, and reprinted in Pugh, DS [Ed] (1971) *Organizational Theory,* Harmondsworth: Penguin

Likert, R (1967) *The Human Organization,* Tokyo: McGraw-Hill Kogakusha

Lucas, H C (1985) *The Analysis, Design and Implementation of Information Systems,* New York: McGraw-Hill

McCormick, E J and Ilgen, D (1985) *Industrial And Organizational Psychology,* London: Allen and Unwin

McEnery, J and McEnery, J M (1987) 'Self-rating in Managerial Training Needs Assessment: a Neglected Opportunity', in *Journal of Occupational Psychology,* Vol 60, pages 49–60

Mager, R F and Pipe, P (1976) *Criteria-Referenced Instruction: Analysis, Design and Implementation,* California: Mager Assoc

Newstrom, J W (1987) 'HRD and the Rule of Four' in *Training,* September, 1987

Pearlman, K (1980) 'Job Families: a Review and Discussion of their Implications for Personnel Section', in *Psychological Bulletin,* Vol 87, pages 1–18.

Pell, C (1989) 'Forward Planning is the Way Through the Funding Jungle', in *Transition,* January, 1989

Phillips, J J (1983) *Handbook of Training Evaluation and Measurement Methods,* Houston: Gulf Publishing

Rowbottom, R (1977), *Social Analysis,* London: Heinemann

Spencer, L M (1986) *Calculating Human Resource Costs and Benefits,* New York: John Wiley

Stewart, D (1986) *The Power Of People Skills,* New York: John Wiley

de Vaus, D A (1986) *Surveys in Social Research,* London: Allen and Unwin

Yammarino, F, Dubinsky, A and Hartley, S (1987) 'An Approach for Assessing Individual Versus Group Effects in Performance Evaluations', in *Journal of Occupational Psychology,* Vol 60, pages 157–67

Index